THE COMPLEXITIES OF BUSINESESS & LIFE COME FROM WITHIN

IT'S JUST

RETAIL

ROGER TYLER

IT'S JUST RETAIL!

THE COMPLEXITIES OF
BUSINESS & LIFE
OFTEN COME FROM WITHIN.

THE COMPLEXITIES OF BUSINESESS & LIFE COME FROM WITHIN

IT'S JUST

RETAIL

ROGER TYLER

"Still Waters – Run Deep"

Cover / Book Design by: ROGER L. TYLER

Dedication

I dedicate this book to my family, mentors, colleagues and coworkers, who have always been there to inspire me to do greater things. I give a very special heartfelt acknowledgment to my loving wife Renee, who has always reminded me that if it were easy, I couldn't be extraordinary. To those special friends and clients who were in search of the *RIGHT BALANCE* in your professional and personal lives and sought my assistance as a means of stability. I am especially grateful that all of you took the time and shared your journeys through retail and life's learning opportunities with me.

What lies behind us and what lies before us are tiny matters compared to what lies within us.

-Henry David Thoreau-

CONTENTS

CONTENTS

CONTENTS

Introduction

W e are all guilty at one time or another of falling victim to dogmatic assertions that have stood the test of time. Because the world around us progressed at a snail's pace ten to fifteen years ago, the assertions had relevance and staying power. By blindly following a single point of view as a conclusion, we often times are making a business or personal situation more difficult to resolve than was truly necessary. We unconsciously look beyond the simplistic and focus on the sophisticated resolutions, as we are sometimes directed. We have a tendency to over engineer a remedy to a situation when our goals and efforts should always remain on achieving simplicity.

I believe this happens sometimes because we, as twenty-first century human beings, crave guidance and resist inaugural change. It is far safer to remain in a group along a beaten path than to be the trailblazer who must endure the trials, tribulations and consequences. And then sometimes it's simply because we didn't take the time necessary to think through the issue well enough to make a better, less complicated judgment and resolve to the situation.

Whichever the case may be, our conscious thoughts and efforts are highly impressionable and require a certain amount of focus and nurturing daily. By nature, the majority of people truly want to follow a leader, a maverick or someone who just makes sense at that time. When most people are left to their own devices, they tend to create overwhelming lists of the things they would like to improve or change in their professional and personal lives. It is usually during this period of reflecting on the vastness of our to-do lists that we go in search of quick all encompassing answers. From whom the answers are derived or the originating basis for the answers is no longer as important as is the acquisition of such for our resolve.

The list itself is a great start, but it is just the beginning. The art of the list is done once it's developed and scribed, now the introduction of the science is needed to segregate, prioritize and timeline the list through completion. One issue at a time should be the focus with the least arduous item first with a reasonable amount of time to resolve. We love to multi-task and try to accomplish more with less time, and that's fine when you are doing chores. But when you are dealing with human emotions, behaviors, business and prosperity; you need to focus.

Our subconscious minds will tend to succumb to the many voices and teachings from a contaminated or negative surrounding. Because our daily diet of unabashed and sensationalized news from the Internet, television and one of our oldest mediums, radio, it has become almost impossible to distinguish fact from fiction. So it is important to maintain as pure of a conscious balance against the pessimism in your day as you possibly can. Even if you just take fifteen minutes each day, and interject a positive counterpoint like: *this too shall pass.*

Try to make this a habit and remember that *the greater good comes as a mighty tide, not in shallow waves.* Soon you will easily ignore the constant distraction of the obligatory waves, and ride the mighty tide of rationalism and pragmatic behavior that can ensure you achieve your goals and expectations. Like most of you, I had searched far and wide during my early formidable years of business asking others and observing conducts so that I may obtain guidance and wisdom. It was later in life, after I began to ignore the superficial waves and ride with the magnanimous tide that I found such answers had to be sought from within.

This book illustrates commonly found business and life situations and the underlying true meaning of solid communications. Most of the time we are unaware of the impact that the constant bombardment of seemingly little negative things have on our subconscious mind. We tend to get caught up in the moment of living our lives as existence, and forget to truly live our lives. You will find some of the messages repeated more than once throughout the book. I am a firm believer that repetition is the mother's milk of retained knowledge. The more you are exposed to something, the more common it becomes to you and the more comfortable you are dealing with it.

The information and examples you're about to read played an important role in bringing harmony to my personal and professional life. By choosing to expand your horizons and see beyond today, I know they'll do the same for you. As you read and reflect on your own life and personal endeavors, you'll discover a foundation for resolving many of your issues and most pressing questions. I have found, and truly believe that the best way to improve any situation is to first recognize you are not alone, choose a strategy for success that works with the resources YOU have, and then execute your strategy with conviction.

It will be my pleasure to assist you through the pages and chapters in this book to recognize, address and alleviate the subtle danger signs that are evident in our everyday lives. You'll be better prepared to identify where substantive communications are anemic, and where communication lacks, chaos soon ensues. You will distinguish some of the most basic principles involved in communicating business processes and relationships as I take you through a roleplaying saga I call; "The Daily Grind" in chapters (6,11 & 19).

Introduction

In some of these excerpts I have taken some
creative licenses in depicting office situations,
relationships and business etiquette. However, in
other daily grind stories the scenes are verbatim
to their actual occurrences. Some of the
characters in this book are fictional, others are
real...you know who you are. The "Daily Grind"
chapters are intended to give a light hearted and
surreal view of the dynamics and relationships in
the retail corporate environment today. With the
knowledge of their existence, you will be better
prepared to launch a counter offensive when you
are faced with a similar situation.

In the adjoining chapters of the book I will
provide some well-documented strategic insights
and basic business principles and processes. My
hope is that you will find them artistically helpful
in establishing and running your chosen area in
business, as well as your personal daily life more
efficiently and, with confidence. We will also
examine and evaluate techniques and quantum
mathematical aspects that have been applied to
technology to allow for more prudent business
decisions.

The goal is for you to gain understanding of
yourself, those around you and how you can
control your destiny by recognizing the past and
using that knowledge to influence the present.
You will diagnose that it takes more than
willpower to overcome failed attempts to secure
change in your life as well as in business. This
is especially evident when the cultures and habits
around you consistently remain the same. You

Introduction

will be charged, educated and ready to differentiate life's circumstances from life's decisions.

It's not about the hand you're dealt; it's how you inevitably play the hand.

I have (25+) academic and practical years of Executive Retail and Consulting Exposure, Experience and Expertise. Crafted and honed in the Department, Dollar, Mass, Specialty, Clothing and E-Commerce areas with some of the most prominent and diverse retailers. I learned from some of the best and brightest and obtained a compulsiveness to teach those willing to grow without limitations. My teams throughout my career have been vast, inspiring and reflective of positive thinkers with the right attitude. I share these teachings with you throughout this book along with personal and professional relationships that congeal to show the different, yet oddly similar aspects of everyday life; and a peculiar yet satisfying symbiotic existence called:

RETAIL!

Chapter 1

Traditional Thinking
Gone with the new economic times!

Traditional thinking in business and life, without argument, has been the cornerstone of our forefather's goals and objectives. As they dredged an empirical path through the most complex issues of their times, it was this style of thinking that continuously proved honorable and sustainable. Many of their final decisions, which then became rules, were predicated on the emotional and ethical foundation of their theological beliefs. And thus they were time tested and impervious to moderate shifts in thinking and behaviors.

Today's business and personal environments no longer are steeped in the honors, traditions and ethical standards once regarded as rock solid. Now, I am not announcing that those standards are completely absent in our society today. I'm just saying that things are somewhat different. There is a noticeably transgressed weighting being applied to the emotional, ethical and spiritual foundation of decisions. Where we once honored traditions, we now evaluate short-term socioeconomic impacts and their affects on the highest-ranking issues of the day. No one institution or entity is clearly better or worse than another on any given

Sunday, although you will hear more about the largest offenders and therefore could easily conjure a different perspective.

The organizations that have survived what we are calling the worst economic conditions seen in this country for decades have not done so because their leaders *hoped* for a better tomorrow. The leaders of these organizations left traditional thinking behind and inspired their teams, controlled their fears, analyzed all opportunities and capitalized on implementing the right personnel and the right technology to manage their assets. Grant it, there is some value of *luck* in the equation of survival over these recent years. Not all organizations that failed in the past few years did so due to ineffective management. But I am not a firm believer in the power of luck. I welcome its' presence, but do not rely on it as a plan.

If you or your organization have not yet taken advantage of this lull in the economy to strengthen your personnel, technology and relationships; then get ready for the trials and tribulations that will come in the next few years from a rapidly changed consumer base and mindset. The ultimate birth of a new consumer is upon us, they have witnessed inventory liquidations, store closings, value pricing and customer friendly associate transformations from your competition…and they like it.

As we awaken from these excessively reported yet no less tumultuous times, I can't help but to wonder what will be the ultimate conclusion. Will people respond positively to the warmth of a new normal in late 2014 and early 2015 or will their surroundings simply absorb them? I can readily envision that some of us will reflect graciously on the gains and lessons learned from our current situation, while the majority of others will only remember the pain and agony of the mistakes made. These defeatists will be narrow in their vision of the future, and only prepare their minds for the next defeat. Not all the changes that have happened or have yet to happen are as gloomy and self-deprecating as we continuously hear from the mainstream media on an almost daily basis.

There are some remarkably positive prospects that have been made available to a much broader audience that were once only available to a select few. In the not so distant future, and by that I am talking in the next 5 years, we will reflect on these times of our lives as the window of opportunity to change and accept change in lockstep with our evolutionary economic environment. But many of you will fail to raise your heads as individuals to see this opportunity. Instead you will choose to be motivated by the issue of the day and continue to wait for a better tomorrow along with the masses.

Changing quickly and on queue to a particular stimulus is not easy, nor is it something for the masses. You have the choice to be a leader of your tomorrow, to do so you must create a foundation for growth and fulfillment by embracing change today. Or you can choose to be what traditional thinking typically exudes, which is to stay docile, exploitable and conditioned to be satisfied with where you are in life. Our circumstances may have brought us here together; however, our individual convictions and the decision to change our behaviors will lead us to our next journey.

It is during some of the most trying times in history that we have allowed ourselves to be corralled into a common way of viewing the situations. In reality it is during these times that many of the existing opportunities are made available to the majority of people if they truly want it. Although the magnitudes of the paradigm shifts in our economy have been substantial, the changes didn't happen overnight. It took a little over a decade for the totality of our current situation to fully play out and become a national tragedy. Some of our leaders and fellow congressional Americans chose not to recognize the imminent dangers of our comfortable spend and barrow trajectory. Others were easily convinced by greed and innocence to take a bite out of the proverbial apple and were helpless against those creating an irrational utopia for society.

That which was recently codified as normal in our lives has changed forever. In some instances the magnitude of such and not the practice has changed. Like saving money diligently for your retirement, living within your financial means and employer-employee loyalty have now become abnormal. This is mostly a reflection of how much the minds and hearts of Americans have been changed for the worse at the speed of the toxic information that was disseminated across our airways. The market crash, layoffs, unemployment and the constant bureaucratic and political party fighting have given cause for such disinclination, especially amongst our youth.

What once was shocking and astonishing privileged information to us a mere five years ago have now become everyday front-page illustrations. T.V. headlines, Internet broadcasts, TMZ reports and innuendos have now become accepted at face value and are now the new normal. In the coming months and years Americans will grow even more agile and comfortable with these seemingly radical changes. Their focus will be on immediate survival and rapid change, which will replace their more supercilious dreams of a better tomorrow for those who follow in our wake; *and then comes tomorrow.*

Patience for most will no longer be a virtue; it will be a sorely missed relic in a viral society that once respected authority, stopped to think before they spoke, or took solace in **not** knowing more than was necessary about someone or something. Although our transition to this new normal feels to be more severe than the changes in past, I would venture to guess that it has similarities to the conditional transitions endured through the late 60's and early 70's. The changes may have been just as severe for them when compared to the *normal* situations of those times. Obviously there are some fairly substantial discords. For instance, during those times our nation wasn't as privileged with the incredible advancements in technology and unending flow of information. Nor were our individual core values so openly announced and distant from one another in what we envisioned at the time to be a well-tuned democratic society.

Or is it all relative to the times that we live in?

Over the last twenty-five years of my professional career and life I have witnessed greatness and tragedy, technological marvels and industrious calamities, personal suffering and triumphs. Through all the experiences, a quality of life was always held true to my foundation and principles. While many of my fellow colleagues basked in the glory of our quarterly accomplishments during the heydays of yesteryears, I found myself continuously questioning whether the results obtained were by happenstance or the results of a well thought out and executed plan. As with most things in life, we tend not to question the good and devote a disproportionate amount of our time and resources reflecting on the bad.

I have had the great fortune to participate in the architecture and engineering of some of the most unique, complex and rewarding business and retail structures in existence today. I have also had the great misfortune of delivering termination notices to some of the most dedicated and loyal associates during a downsizing and occasional demise of otherwise healthy businesses. Through no fault of their own, sometimes these trustworthy associates became pawns of an organization's self-righteous and self-contained leadership.

What you have to recognize and believe in is the fact that you can *only* control things that are truly under your control. By that I mean you can't make, wish or hope that in due time things will eventually go as planned if someone else has a controlling part in the plan. Nor do you have the ability to control or change people as often as you may have thought. You have to take the responsibility to set reasonable expectations and allot an appropriate amount of time for resolution. When that time has elapsed, follow through on your secondary goals or plans.

Observing corporations through our often rose-colored glasses, we sometimes view them as entities of excellence, and embodiments of imperialistic thought processes of intellectually advanced teams. The reality is that most organizations are really nothing more than a team of people structured together by many levels of management to accomplish a sometimes-common goal.

As in our common everyday lives, we sometimes forget the value of our existence is dependent on and directly correlated to our value of relationships. When we combine our individual efforts just right in a team setting, the results are truly amazing. We should and actually do depend on others more than you may realize. Take your everyday life for example. Even if you live alone, you depend on the utility company to supply your household functional necessities, the grocery store for sustenance and the gas station for the fuel that enables your transportation. The same holds true for organizations, although there is typically resistance to acknowledge the symbiotic relationships by juxtaposing business units, each group has a functional reliance and responsibility to and with the other.

I was fortunate to have recognized this seemingly common aspect early in my career and made it a point to seek out and engage leadership and associates with intellect and positive attitudes. Through teamwork, effort and proper vision we collectively created value for the consumers, harmony with the associates and respect from the competition. I am going to share something that just may surprise you.

As I commandeered executive leadership roles with leading organizations, there was rarely a direct correlation between the size of a company's resources and their ability to achieve a high rate of success. You might think that the basic logic for success or failure would come down to the amount of risk, or better yet, the amount of risk management an entity or person deploys. You would be wrong. I am sorry to be the bearer of such truths, but risk reward ratios are statistically inept at governing success. We will elaborate on this subject at another time. But suffice it to say that risk tolerance is more of a conditional reaction and not an intellectual one.

Think of it this way and then we'll move on. If you have the resources and wherewithal to acquire all the top students from the top Ivy League schools you have only exasperated your risk ratio, not alleviated it. Here's an example of what I am describing to you. The intellectual powers that be for Lehman Brothers, a now defunct financial services firm, utilized substantially advanced teams of scholarly education and prowess. They spent fortunes on understanding and calculating risks, but they failed to recognize that they highly compensated individuals on high returns, which in itself were dependent on high risks and induced a conditional reaction.

The most common themes for success and happiness come down to two critical aspects in an organization and the organizing of your life, people and vision. During my career as an executive decision maker in diverse multi-billion dollar retail organizations and start-ups alike, the keys for success are often in the hands of the ill prepared. I can honestly tell you that I learned *what to do* in crisis situations from some of the best and brightest executive leaders that the industry has to offer, and *what NOT to do* from some of the worst.

First, the number one reason for the segregation of success and failure amongst businesses of similar genre, commodity and size can be broken down into three words; PEOPLE, PEOPLE & PEOPLE. Now I'm not talking about the number of, intellect of, or collective background experiences of the people in the company. No, the basic guiding principle of sustained success and continuous improvements is ATTITUDE. The past couple of years have been marked as some of the most tumultuous times for businesses and people alike. Unfortunately I predict that we will not see meaningful recovery until 2014. You will see stagnation as we push through the Presidential elections of 2012. The early part of 2013 will be filled with opinions and innuendos of what coulda-shoulda-woulda; leaving the later part of 2013 and early 2014 for recovery focus. However, the challenge is not what has happened to us, but what we will do to create a better tomorrow. The same can pretty much be said about the health of your relationships and how you function as a human being. It isn't the *quantity* of friends you have accumulated on Facebook or your Twitter account or the number of email addresses...it is the *quality* of those friends that will enrich your life.

Unlike today's more common measurement of being befriended by a host of individuals online, traditional thinking would dictate that *affiliation does not a friend make*. In other words, communicating with a true friend does not always involve talking or chatting. In fact, your measurement of true friendship resides in the comfort of knowing that when silence comes and you grow your individual lives separately, you do this without growing apart. When this becomes your measurement of success, you will have taken the pebble from the hand.

Successful individuals and companies have chosen to communicate their intentions both internally and externally with a focus on the possibilities for tomorrow not the issues. Those who are truly preparing for these new economies are not hunkering down, no; they continue to push the envelope to ensure that they at least double the project and process failure rate to the previous year. That's right, you read that correctly, *double* the **FAILURE** rate. When failures occur, learning is happening. Growth is then a mere by-product of rationalized mistakes and success is an inevitable outcome. When coupled with the right attitude towards mistakes, the foundation for accelerated growth becomes an infectious determination and desire within the teams.

Second, a widely misconstrued business and personal mantra in existence today that heavily contributes to the rate of success and failure is VISION. Many unsuccessful companies proclaim their vision as something tangible, something that will accomplish a means to the end of their decreed destination. They tend to place this vision in their corporate mantra, and to obtain their vision certain steps must be accomplished in succession. I have found that the most successful organizations, as well as the people running them, recognize their vision not as a tangible asset or solidified goal, but as an emotional or spiritual-like entity.

{Making and keeping associates happier than their customers, will ensure loyalty from the team and satisfaction from the consumer.}

Some organizations and individuals alike fail to realize that their vision, mantra or mission statements are only affective when they conjure a genuine feeling in all who internalize it. Most have converted to the sole use of a mantra, which should be reduced to as few words as possible and yet capable of creating transformation among all members of the organization. Some examples of effective and easily adapted mantras for different entities are; "healthy fast food" for a restaurant, "Performance On Deck" for a sports retailer, "Women's Lives Enriched" for the multitude of retailers who cater to specific genders, and my personal favorite for everyday living…"Budgeted Expectations, Surpassed."

This emotional driver will ultimately consecrate the hearts and minds of the associates and guide the organization by desire to succeed. By creating an ongoing desire and not a finish line, you thus emulsify the team's coordinated efforts with a genuine will to succeed. If Mary in the mailroom or Mike at the receptionist desk cannot quickly, without hesitation recite your mantra with a smile and conviction…you've missed the boat.

To ensure success, in business as well as in your everyday life, you need honest, straightforward communications. I know it sounds so simple, but it is so elusive for so many of us. **Consistent** communications are the foundation to understanding differences of opinions, objectives and relationships. That which is not said, often is never executed. How many times have you heard, or even mentioned yourself, *{…that goes without saying…}*? The truth is, you **need** to say it, hear it, read it and repeat it. Communication is not a one-way ordeal; the effort of oral or written dictation warrants a response. Not because of etiquette or formality of it, but for clarification and refinement if need be. Without an open forum of communication in your life, you will continue to find roadblocks to your life/work balance and tranquility.

Businesses are made up of people, and people have idiosyncrasies that often defy our ability to fully understand them. I illustrate some common examples in this book that will assist you in developing your inner ability to first recognize the issue, alleviate the excuses and blame, and formulate an actionable resolution. Just as we are trained in our early years of life to believe that certain actions will cause instant and measurable reactions, so can we learn how to avoid environments that will produce unwanted actions. The foundation of the first couple of chapters is designed to enhance your business and personal repertoire of sustainable, proactive course correcting measures. These measures will enable you to confidently engage in business and personal conversations where you will be providing preemptive counseling as opposed to the more common reactive issue resolutions.

I hope that you enjoy your journey with me through the pages of this book. I promise that if you keep an open mind you will encompass a combination of the science, the art and the seldom-recognized *human conditional responses* in the arena of retail as well as life in general.

No matter what your spiritual, emotional or religious beliefs, you will recognize and determine your life's ambitions through the upcoming pages. Pay particularly close attention to the chapters focused on your mind's natural ability to have victory over fear. You will gain natural acceptance and abilities to monitor, recognize and react to your own balanced signals from your heart, soul and mind. The chapters of this book will engage you in a process of awareness that will empower you to adopt the fact that those around you do **NOT** determine your purpose in life; your purpose in life will determine the people who are around you.

IT'S JUST RETAIL!

Chapter 2

What Got Us Here, Won't Keep Us Here

We rarely need to be reminded of the hard work, perseverance and sacrifice that it took for us to achieve a goal. Whether it was losing weight, a score on a final exam, the competition preparation as an athlete, or creating a financial roadmap towards prosperity. Each of us has the right to claim victory over our own challenge, by our own standards without being compared to someone or something else. But if we don't utilize some measuring stick, or universal form of standardization, how will we know if our progress is adequate, subpar or well above average? Now that the goal has been achieved, how do you maintain your position or progress to the next level? As a person, this decision is yours and yours alone to make. You can be perfectly content with where you are, whom you're with and how you live. As a company you are fiducially bound by your organization and the associates therein to produce incremental results, thus staying where you are or heaven forbid, digressing is not an option.

People are often compelled by others to "push-on" or "dig deeper" even when we are exhausted both physically and mentally. It is during these times that our minds and bodies will produce and release endorphins that make us feel fatigued, drowsy and sometimes dissolution. These are alerts designed by nature and are regulatory in function for your welfare. They are your indicators to stop, rest and take control of an exhaustive situation and bring balance back into your life. As you may well know, or at the very least been told, you can gain strength and fortitude by focusing on and overcoming a consistent physical or mental stumbling block. What you may not know is that by ignoring your internal alarms you are also weakening your ability to recognize the signals to balance your life.

You don't always have to rearrange your schedule and sacrifice your needs to ensure that you can make things better for those around you. Spend as much or more time figuring out what will make things better for you. Your company prospers when it is full of excited, energized personnel who believe in what they do and enjoy doing a great job. You become one of those people by listening and reacting to your needs. Where you are today is only the step needed to get you to where you want to go. Keep that in mind as you continue your journey.

Sometimes you have to step back and remind yourself that *it's just retail*, and your life, love and family should take precedence over the waves of daily issues. Concentrate on that which will provide you with a solid return on your time and intellectual investment. Shun the creed from those around you who consistently deem just about every situation as cataclysmic. Everything that is deemed an issue isn't a critical one all the time. Many people hang on to the memories that their ability to meticulously evaluate every aspect of their job and find ways to make it better drove their passion. However, that deep dive analysis into all aspects of your job and life won't get you to the next level. A more global perspective and ability are usually more beneficial at each upper level of management and maturity through life. What got you this far will not necessarily carry you any further, nor will it sustain your current position. It was a necessary foundation builder, but it is not a scalable practice and no longer serves your aspirations and those who depend on your growth.

The tides of business and life most often will shift against us when we allow ourselves to be influenced by our fears and inhibitions in unfamiliar surroundings. The pursuit of harmony becomes complicated when we try to artificially straddle the pressures from one faction of our personal and business lives by sacrificing the balance of the others. For instance, many people have chosen to overly commit themselves to the pure business or work aspect of their lives in pursuit of an illustrious career. They do this with the intent that they will enjoy the fruits of their labor later in life. They tend to be impervious to the fact that many of the superficial relationships that are seemingly flourishing in their life are business induced, and have no genuine real life meaning behind them. The artificial fruits of their labor are instant and fulfill a yearning to succeed and feel good today, but are short lived and rarely cherished, and then on to the next conquest they go. It's the quick fixes that seem to sustain those in search of emotional gratification today...*and then comes tomorrow.*

As you take stock in the world we live in and the everyday happenings around you, stop a minute to recognize that what was once *nice* to know about something or someone just a few short years ago has now transformed into an immediate *need* to know. Our thirst for information in this new era has become a borderline obsession. This obsession to know more, and to know it first has produced extreme anxiety among a large portion of our population. Just think about what you heard, saw or read from the mainstream media just a few short years ago. It was dignified, credible and generally bias in its delivery. Today, and I hate to think of tomorrow, we hear, see and read things that are completely unfounded, unrehearsed and subject to hearsay at best in many cases. This dilemma is exciting, and frightening at the same time. Sublime knowledge at the speed of Internet has its rewards, but can be a burden on a society that isn't quite mature enough to handle it.

The magnificent transformation from what was once a comfortable ignorance of things around us; to a ten-second Google search for verification of the very origin of those things; has opened an entirely new dynamic and complexity to our daily lives. We are witnessing the evolution of readily available abundant information that was typically a commodity retained by a few intellectuals with sophisticated equipment. It is now available to a Four year old and is considered a disposable commodity. You can take in all you want with a stroke of a finger or a few spoken words into a device's microphone. This conversion hasn't been easy for a lot of people, but change worth doing wasn't meant to be easy. I don't believe that anyone truly wants to constrain the access to this information; the use of such however is a genuine concern. The truth is not always delivered; it often has to be sought.

Some of the results of this instant gratification societal swing are that the term "WE" has become "I" and the needs of many are inconsequential to the wants of the few. No longer is the foundation and historical accomplishments of the company's namesake as important as the stock price today or the adjoining size of the executive bonus payouts tomorrow. Under these keystone environments you quickly discover that the company no longer belongs to everyone; it soon belongs to no one.   Once the swashbuckling buccaneers and corporate raiders drain the coffers of an organization, they are off to their next victim. It is within these types of scenarios that I feel the most empathy for the associates. Many of who are naïve to the objectives of the very people they hope to be saviors of their jobs and livelihood.

The associates are rarely communicated to and often are given false hope as business conditions deteriorate and the executives prepare themselves for evacuation with their Golden Parachutes.   I particularly remember those associates who were prepared to *"do whatever it takes"* to secure their future with a floundering business, even when the business structure was collapsing around them. It was during those darkest, most challenging times that I witnessed the power of laser-focused leadership and how practical rationalization echoes through the halls creating a calm responsive business structure.

Unlike what you may have heard previously in your life, you do not always have to play the hand that you were dealt. Sometimes you can lay your cards down, start over and create a new foundation for your new destiny. Hope and wishing have been unequivocally denounced as official game plans; *feel free to pass this little tidbit along.* Looking for someone or something to create your path to prosperity for you will all but ensure your failure. One of my favorite and most simple secrets to success and controlling your destiny is accepting guidance, not requesting instructions. Accept the wisdom from others and apply it to the way you work the best. Do not ask for a complete step-by-step roadmap when the process is totally foreign to you. Obstacles will appear from time to time and will require your utmost attention. You must learn from yesterday's obstacles, work through today's obstacles, and prepare for tomorrow's obstacles. Although you are in control of your destiny, you accomplish more in a group and can flourish as a team when you focus on results, not the academics of the process.

Retail, relationships and life in general are more complicated now than ever before. Or is it that we continue to make things more complicated than they actually need to be? Lest we forget that even in today's tumultuous environment, the ultimate achievement in our lives is defined by our ability to strike a harmonious balance between work, family, love and life. The simplicity of achieving this balance is intrinsic to our very nature. Our strengths and abilities come from within our hearts, souls and minds if we allow them to cohesively flourish naturally and uninhibited by our fears.

Just as your mind naturally and unconsciously will invoke you to feed your body with nutrients when it is hungry, take on fluids when it is thirsty; love when it is reciprocated and rest when it is exhausted; it will also naturally balance you unconsciously when stress ensues. The trouble with most people is that they tend to disregard the signals provided by the rhythms of our subconscious minds and bodies to create a natural work life balance. Most often it is because they follow the paths of others or are directed by someone else as to what's best for them.

We are often paralyzed by fear within our professional and personal lives. Fear is good; it was designed as the foundational function towards self-preservation. Too little of it, and you'll find trouble in your path. Too much, and you'll find trouble following your path. The illustrations and information contained herein will provide you with the groundwork by which you will gain a perspective on your most paralyzing fears. Once you are able to identify and contain the majority of those fears, the residual inhibitions will soon become vacant memories. By taking a step back and recognizing that you are a human being first and an associate of an organization second, your horizons and perspectives will flourish.

Most of us are very similar in our quest for rationalization; we are often taken a back when the words or mannerisms used are easily misinterpreted. Asking questions is fundamental to learning and fear of doing so creates a vacuum for many wrong ideological ideas to flourish. Lets face it, change is inevitable and every one of us should embrace the future with the power of knowledge and understanding. The alternative is to succumb to the very winds of change that are designed to propel you. But, because you are afraid to raise your sails in today's unfamiliar world, you remain static.

HAVE WE COME/GONE TOO FAR?

In a recent poll, 85% of respondents felt that the world's progression due to the information revolution was hands down much faster today than in the past. Now, if you're like me you know that polls have an inherent flaw in providing the surface information. What if most of the respondents were too young or less informed to recognize that it wasn't that long ago that out nation went through an industrial revolution that sparked a similar impact? Our professional and personal lives have become more entwined than we may have realized through this revolution of late. The sheer numbers of people who recite statements about what they heard, or thought they heard are blurring the distinction between knowledge and gossip. Today's media has fostered a new standard of reciprocating information that no longer has to be proofed or validated. The more sensationalized the story, the faster it will make our many media waves. We are rapidly realizing that not every sound bite heard is the very thing that changes our lives dramatically and forever.

However, you must realize that your level of adaptation to your continuously evolving surroundings comes into direct correlation with your ability to thrive and prosper in today's new normalcy. Your *attitude,* more so than your *intellect,* will dictate the level of progress you achieve navigating the complexities of the future. The level of enrichment to your mind that you accept, will govern the proliferation of the collective knowledge of those around you. Stretching your knowledge capacity in ways that weren't even available a mere five years ago will enable you to become more relevant in our ever-changing society and its rules of engagement.

The speed at which today's technology will evolve and impact our lives of tomorrow will be mind boggling to say the least. With these changes will be an ever-increasing level of astonishment, distrust, confusion and segregation. You can choose to master your domain, or become a slave to it, but it will change and progress...your challenge will be to acknowledge and remember that you're in a marathon; not a sprint.

As we indulge our minds with the latest breaking news reports, alerts and email blasts, we must all pause to recognize that information travels unbridled in today's society. Whether factual or sensationalized, we tend to gobble it up and disseminate *the facts as we heard them* amongst our adoptive *tribes* at work, on YouTube, Facebook, Twitter, LinkedIn, Blogs and any other social media available.   This communication phenomenon is unlike the early days in retail when we began to fully utilize the capabilities of the *contraption* called the personal computers or PC for short.   There was far less social capacity and interconnectivity between our "minute by minute" lives and our work performance for the day. You could not answer a question about your competitors or gain insight to the day's market value with the click of a mouse.

And yet we were mesmerized by the available information conjured from the early renditions of the Internet, and relied less and less on our green screen computer terminals that could only engage us through a stagnant mainframe environment. Those of us that can remember when; recall that then too were the defectors who warned of retail urban plight and cursed the world that chose to type in a spreadsheet rather than to handwrite in a daily ledger.

For 'tis the act of writing the printed sales numbers and inventory facts from one sheet to another that compels the mind to retain the information that was being scribed.
  "Ancient retail leaders 10.1 commandments"

With the onset of these expansive new computer appliances came the ability, and soon thereafter the requirement to question all that was once held as true based on a person's word or the printed report in front of you.

From a retail perspective, in most recent years this has spawned a fast growing regiment in retail of **ERP** business operating solutions. **E**nterprise **R**esource **P**lanning quickly became the mantra for the retail industry. The idea of having one unified system that integrates all of a corporation's unique business routines from planning and accounting, to operations and fulfillment gained tremendous traction in the late 90's.

Most of the systems were based on consumer centric demand patterns, quantum mathematics and homogeneously infused forecast engines. These modules were, and are still today touted as being able to predict and guide companies to utopia in the retail sector. Executives couldn't place their orders for the latest renditions fast enough. Every quarter flaunted the birth of a new ERP system that was uniquely designed to resolve your most pressing business issues. Each new system was more robust and complicated than its' predecessor and guaranteed to resolve your issue *du jour*. And oh, by the way, as the salesperson would not hesitate to inform you, it is also being shown to your competition as we speak; so who is going to get the competitive edge?

Many leaders wouldn't even entertain a discussion unless the system that was being presented had a list of competitors currently using it. Talk about trying to *keep up with the Joneses*! Whatever happened with differentiation, and cutting edge, and being creative? Nope, the basic mantra was that *I'll have what they're having* and yet we'll expect different results. Thus began the journey into *Retail Insanity* by many of the most prevalent corporations and their executive leaders.

During the last decade and a half I have copiously studied the fundamentals and causes of some of the most complex business issues. My studies have carried me from small start-ups to the multi-billion dollar organizations. I have worked with some of the most noted intellectually and technologically advanced business teams and software vendors in the industry. We have collaborated to develop systems, processes and policies to alleviate mundane tasks and process regiments that have impeded the progress of the business units we engaged. Today I can tell you that 85% of the systems implemented 3 to 5 years ago are now either obsolete or function at a level far less than imagined. It's not the systems; generally it comes down to the processes and people.

Early on, during my trials and tribulations, I recognized the immediate and profound correlation between sustainable sound business resolutions and those that are quick, cheap and based on the myopic issues of today. Surprisingly, the differentiator between fixes and resolutions was not within the acumen of the associates. In fact, the personnel at most of the corporations that I worked with were very similar in their levels of knowledge. Most associates, and many of the secondary level leaders were exceptionally knowledgeable about **what** they do for their company.

The issue became evident when the question posed centered on **why** they did what they did. Very few associates, and leaders for that matter, could rapidly and fluidly illustrate the means to their efforts. Now this would not be a surprise in a tactical operation that was task oriented, like a factory production line. However, there is no place for this mindless execution in retail. The rapid evolution of the consumer's shopping habits and tastes requires new and fresh approaches almost daily.

It was once a belief of mine that a company was only as strong as the personnel they hired, trained and retained. Poised, aggressive, rigidly focused leaders will get the job done best. Without intellectually advanced personnel to lead the masses, the results of any corporate campaigned would be constrained and destined to fail at meeting the global objectives. I no longer subscribe to that myth. I have consistently proven that when you encourage average intelligence personnel to express their ideas and inspire passion for what they're doing, they consistently exceed their intellectually advanced cohorts in performance. Each organization that I have worked with has relied on me to simplify their processes and attune their personnel to a new system, direction, policy and/or procedure. To take a company forward, you must first acknowledge and understand the past. Seek those who are key in their business units and communicate with clarity your role, expectations and commitment to their success.

The core to my finding of what went wrong, and how to fix it had less to do with the intellectual prowess of the associates. It centered more towards the process by which the issues were being addressed. Many times it came down to the directives employed by the executive team. What I found might not surprise some of you, but I am sure it will provide you with better insight. What is more important, I will illustrate some everyday remedies to alleviate the stress and uncertainty that paralyzes so many people from doing the right thing consistently.

A corporate entity is a part of a more complex operational society, and with that basis of understanding comes the wisdom as a leader to change feelings first, then attitudes and finally you can change the mind. The everyday forces that drive typical human responses outside of the workplace, are often the very same that are used inside the workplace. People are generally sensitive to the same triggers and great leaders know how to invoke similar responses of respect, admiration or just plain recognition. Many newly appointed leaders confuse the deliverance of a power title with a need to abuse or degrade subordinates. I have found that most of these leaders, who are guilty of this behavior, have generally been recipients of poor leadership. Some of these poor leaders are of their own making and have no one to blame for their issues. As I would tell many of my associates, *"you are human beings first, employees of this organization second; do not let anyone control your feelings or aptitude by words or expressions."*

My executive retail experiences have taken me through 9 different states where I have taken residence and instituted proper change. I have had the pleasure of implementing and augmenting some 30 different high tech merchandise planning, allocation and procurement systems along side some of the best and brightest PhD's and experts in the retail sector. I have trained and guided more than 250 associates from entry level to vice presidents, and partnered with more than 40 Senior Level Executives across diverse retail establishments to institute deliverable comprehensive strategic goals and objectives.

As diverse as the retailers were that I worked with spanning from specialty to dollar stores, mass retailers to department stores, catalog and mail order, Internet and international, they also had their similarities. Each company exhibited a common theme that proved to be a prohibitory condition to rapidly accelerating revenue growth, and developing quality leadership amongst the associates. With this causal affect identified, I quickly began to formulate course of action that was sustainable and actionable based on my assessment of the personnel and conditions within the four walls of the organization.

The real difference between good leadership and the great accomplished and forward thinking leaders is what I call the **A** factors. These factors are **A**ttitude and **A**tmosphere. The greatest of leaders exude a positive attitude and infuse the associates with a feeling of importance and admiration. When you couple these two factors in a positive way, the results are consistently the same across all business units of a company. Show me a business unit whose leadership has provided a nurturing and supportive business atmosphere; one that the associates are allowed to question directions and suggest improvements; and I will show you a successful diamond in the rough. You can give me an average intelligence team with the right attitude towards accomplishing a goal over a highly educated skilled group of players who have the attitude of individualism and self preservation every time.

How do you find and assemble the former group of individuals? You first have to look within yourself and your leadership team. Do you have the leadership abilities to foster an atmosphere that stimulates and cultivates the minds of your team? Can you recognize and reward individuals while engaging the team's focus on attitude and not intellect? Most leaders today have been programed over the years to do just the opposite. The goals have always been to single out the best and worst performers and make examples of their contributions to the team, all the while allowing mediocrity to flourish amongst the majority of the associates.

To create the best, you have to be at your best. A coach must first recognize that their skills must be seamlessly transferred to their associates. To be truly great in retail, you must be willing to instill greatness in your team. Otherwise, the team will consistently fail and your legacy will be measured accordingly. Continuous process and revenue generating improvements along with quality communications will ensure that the past efforts will not be regarded as a flash in the pan. Change is inevitable, don't allow the fear of taking that first step towards change keep you from achieving your goals and the goals of those around you.

Chapter 3

Fear In The Hearts & Minds Of Retail

Through my years of observation as a consultant and executive in retail, I have witnessed a reoccurring theme among the capricious and conventional business operations. This theme proved to be a very common trait that quite literally prohibited abundant and repeatable success in organizations from ever seeing the light of day. What I found was that the connection between the majority of common business issues, and the level of complexity applied towards resolving the issue had a common characteristic.

I would witness this correlation throughout the entire hierarchy of business units, from the entry-level associates, up and along the ranks and into the executive teams. The often self-constrained business processes created a false sense of accomplishment and thus an unrecognized embrace of mediocrity. The indisputable culprit that was responsible in every incident that I identified permeated from a humanistic primal *fear* of *failure*.

Most businesses do not even come close to their full potential because of this most basic human behavior. Fear of failure is not a characteristic that will allow you or your company to move forward.   To recognize this obstructive behavior, you sometimes need an outside view of your internal processes and code of conduct as it relates to issue resolution.   Using a newly hired associate, or engaging a consultant from time to time is good business practice to unveil the abnormalities within your normal activities. What appears to be business as usual, and normal business etiquette could be immobilizing your company.

Spending an exorbitant amount of time over analyzing a relatively benign issue or consistently taking the safe route can do more harm than you may realize.   Unknowingly you may be the main cause in stifling the creativity and growth potential of the individual associates and teams.   Associates will listen to your words, but will follow your examples. So they learn from your actions when you take the time to interrogate the team regarding an issue of who left the gate open.   Your actions cultivate their minds as they watch and learn.   A more industrious approach might be to solicit ideas on how we can cost effectively engineer a process where the gate will close itself in the future.

Each instance where I was able to identify this behavior, I knew that meaningful repetitious actions were needed sooner rather than later.   To produce results quickly, I focused the attention on the *course* of actions taken to get them where they were, versus the analysis of the obvious outcome rendered.   It isn't always the process used that is wrong, sometimes it's the way the process was executed.

Over time the corporations began to realize that not only did this fear of failure paralyze some of the most capable and brightest superstars in their organization; the punishments for the so-called mistakes endowed mediocrity. Many of the organizations were oblivious to the fact that their negative reactions and lack of recovery directions consumed more energy and resources than celebrating the effort and enjoying a teaching moment. They had to be trained on the premise that if mistakes are met with bold and immediate corrective actions on a consistent basis, the mistakes were invaluable to the team's ability to learn and retain knowledge.

Far too many short-term goals have evolved as the new normal to issue resolution in the minds of many of our retail leaders today. They have forgotten or chosen to dismiss the fact that the confrontation between customer loyalty and customer appreciation is a losing proposition for the company. Pricing and breadth of assortment are evolutionary practices that can hinder loyalty and entice appreciation from on the short side, but have beneficial long-term aspects. Just remember that price is what the customer pays for your offering, loyalty is what you get when you listen and react.

Today's fast paced corporations have lost the objective of governing their team's actions towards long-term goals. Many of the leaders have digressed to the level of micro managing the individual daily issues. There is a void in the retail community, and dare I say our country, of those who are willing to have conviction in their own ability and the abilities of their associates. We need more leaders who are not afraid to try something new and creative. It is this aversion to change that has created a retail society of technicians and rote process personnel. Thinking on their own and cultivating ideas into projects are not encouraged and thus nonexistent in most business units today.

For example, in the procurement divisions their current determination and focus is generally laser guided to resolve a precursor mathematical equation that will, regardless of budget or physical capacity, embrace the 98% accuracy rating of their inventory forecasts. The ability to accurately predict your future outcome does not ensure success of your company. If I bask in the pure arithmetic knowledge that by traveling 60 miles per hour, I will be able to predict my distance from point A to point B in 60 minutes doesn't ensure my direction is correct. Think about it. What has been left behind in our unquenchable thirst for systemic answers is the humanistic value of our customers. The relational and rationalized product assortments based on consumer centric demand patterns and price optimization standards is often controlled by quantum mathematics and not true behavioral patterns.

Far too many senior level executives and managers are afraid to accept responsibility for their actions and thus you hear the terms; *systems issues, weather, too early – too late...etc.,* used time and time again when in reality it was *leadership error.* Many of today's leaders find an enormous amount of discomfort in declaring their true feelings and attitudes towards the somewhat unpredictable onset of a situation. Many of these same leaders however are far too open and willing to chastise others, *after the fact,* regarding decisions made that did not pan out.

They've forgotten, or perhaps were never exposed to the axiom *that it is better to ask forgiveness, than to ask permission* when they are the captains of a project. They would much rather stay close to normal operations, industry best practices and follow a current trend as apposed to creating a new process that is the genesis of a new business or product introduction that creates the trend and emboldens growth.

There was a time, not so long ago, when making mistakes simply meant you were learning. The more abundant they were, the more of life's lessons were learned and to the offender, wisdom and knowledge was embarked. During these what seemingly are now ancient times, forgiveness was a natural outcome from the recipients; *as to err was human, but to forgive was divine.* It was a time when motives were not second-guessed, and the art of communication was paramount to everyone's daily ritual.

Today, mistakes have been taken to a place where they are no longer portals of discovery and evidence of human existence, but are quickly magnified and severely punished. One rarely is afforded the luxury of rebuttal and explanation in response to an untruth; *EVERYONE* loves a good story and the truth often repudiates a good plot. You no longer can rely on what was meant by a statement or action, you are held accountable for what was said and the outcome. As a publicly traded company quickly finds, the analyst and shareholders are relentless on their demands of your hypothetical forecasts. They insist that you obtain answers where there often are none to be found.

...will your sales and profits improve by 25% next quarter? ...do you see your competitors pulling back on inventory investments by 15% or more this year?

If such answers were readily available and more importantly, could be relied upon to come to fruition, you would already have disclosed your expectations and confidently launched your counter offensive. You certainly would not have to undertake the arduous work of compiling rigorous defensive measures and evaluating *what-if* scenarios to ensure relative sales gains and profitability for your organization's fiscal year and beyond. However, analyst and shareholders are people, and they always have and will continue for sometime into the future, *expect* the impossible and *rely* on the improbable... *as long as it makes for a Good Story...* and a healthy return on their investments.

Business leaders have digressed to an existence where it is no longer admirable to disclose a mistake or honor one's fallacies. Once worn as a badge of honor, our confessions to a wrongdoing illustrated strength and resilience in our convictions and principles. In today's retail society a person adorns a scarlet letter for disclosing the reality of a situation, especially where a stretch of the truth would suffice. Some well-qualified and good intentioned leaders have had the audacity to profess truth behind a sales miss or inventory accumulation during a quarter end conference call. When this ambiguous act of treason occurs in the realm of publicly traded retail, you are condemned and offered a place on the wall of shame often times never to be heard from again. Once the board members of an organization have evaluated such subversion amongst their tribe, only the offender's epitaph remains. The following day's press release and/or discussions with the associates embodies the soothing phrase that:

"Ms. Johnson has chosen to step down and immediately relinquish her duties here at The Firm in pursuit of other interests; we wish her the best!"

Of course, let's not forget that there are many close personal and nonprofessional relationships that begin and persevere amongst a shadow of cover-ups and unspoken

truths.   Those who commit such atrocities under the
umbrella of business relationships, are not concerned of a
possible wrong perception. They parade these core vendors
through the organization as if they were a nonprofit
company doing your organization a favor.

Once this snowball of deception begins to roll, the
catastrophe to behold its' true nature *will* occur; it's just a
matter of time. If only the culprits would take a moment to
survey the wake of issues yet to arise from their momentary
lapse in judgment. We may never have heard of Enron,
WorldCom or Bernie Madoff had the frauds being
perpetrated met with a moment of reflection to where their
actions were headed once the illegal acts came to fruition.

Yet, after all we've seen, heard and read in the last few
years some companies continue to evolve themselves and
their followers in a world that conceals mistakes and thus
stifles creativity. Most continue to commit this heinous act
under the umbrella of *"positive news begets positive
reactions"*, even if the positive news is fabricated. For
those of you who wish to make a sustained difference, keep
your associates informed, honesty and integrity are not just
statements and words, they are paramount to the success of
all well run organizations. It doesn't take 100s of people
doing *a few* things well; it takes only a *few* people doing
key performance enhancing things well to achieve success
throughout the organization.

To obtain your team's greatest achievements, they **will** be
preceded by many mistakes.   You must subdue the
irrational and immediate fear of failure in your teams with a
collection of discussions and best practices for them to
follow. To fully enjoy life, relationships and retail; you
cannot succumb to the largest mistake of them all; DOING

NOTHING to save your honor!   You may relinquish that dubious distinction to those who have allowed the simple pleasures of *true* happiness in life to be replaced by ambiguity and narcissism.

The light speed, by which we communicate, get and transmit information, is a double-edged sword on society, business and what we accept as *normal*. The benefits of such scientific accomplishments are enormous and our lives enriched, for the most part. However, retractions are far more difficult to disseminate when a mistake is uncovered. Everyone loves a good story; even if it's not the **whole** story. Unless your organization doesn't currently have or plan to have in the foreseeable future disgruntled associates, you're susceptible to the wrath of Facebook, Twitter and other social media networking outlets. Although we live in a democratic society that has adopted the creed of Innocent until proven guilty, the humanity laws of the social network are only implied, and rest on the doctrine that these written words are the opinions of the user.   In other words, you may choose to believe it or not. In today's world we find that; *the truth has just entered the starting gate as the lie crosses the finish line and is declared*;

WINNER!!

Chapter 4

Whose Mistake Is It?

It was once said to me, in a semi-jokingly manner, that the best way to mitigate a problem is to never make a mistake. Since that is hardly practical, I have found that issues are more readily circumvented using a three-step process.

> "Wise men profit more from fools than fools from wise men; for the wise men shun the mistakes of fools, but fools do not imitate the successes of the wise."[1]

To duplicate an error is criminal, to commit one is human and to resolve one based on obtained or learned knowledge is wise. I have adopted a process to issue resolution that always takes the necessary time between receiving the issue or mistake and announcing or directing the resolution. The best resolutions are actionable and sustainable with focused efforts on the forward motion and not on the backward

---

[1] **Cato the Elder**, *from Plutarch, Lives*
Roman orator & politician (234 BC - 149 BC)

causes. Please recognize that understanding what happened and taking the corrective actions to mitigate the possible reoccurrence of the same mistake in the future is the only way to achieve progress. My simple yet effective three-step process encompasses taking time to *evaluate, examine* and *execute*.

Under these guidelines you will find contentment and fortitude, which are a deadly combination against issues and problems. The time you take to properly address each issue is infinitesimal to the time you will have saved on the backend of short sided, hasty judgments. Sometimes you have to walk away from the past to ensure that you have a clear vision of your future. Don't get caught up in the moment that was, prepare for the moment that will be.

You will find that by ***evaluating*** your circumstances; uncovering the *How-* did this happen, *Who –* does it affect, and *When* can a permanent resolution be initiated. The **How – Who - When** creates a foundation from which you can build your resolution. You may have noticed that there is not a **Why** in my campaign. The reason is that by introducing a **Why**, we tend to focus on attempting to control that which is not ours to do so. **Why** focuses on the source of an issue, or a purpose and reason behind it. Although the argument is compelling to know why something happened, it only holds relevance to the prohibiting of the exact same issue in the future; not dealing with the here and now. The majority of leaders today are clearly more focused on the cause of an issue rather than preparing and deploying a remedy for the issue at hand.

For instance, the aforementioned majorities are concerned about *why* **this** fire started rather than formulating a plan of action and series of responses in the event of **any** fire in the future. What does it matter if lightening, gas leak, wiring or matches started the fire? The focus should be on the responses; dial 911, grab the fire extinguisher, drop to the ground, ensure everyone gets to the neighbors.... etc. The forbearance to succession planning will enable cooler heads to prevail in an emergency, which will always conjure more positive results than the panicked approach.

The same holds true in business when sales are not up to par. Does it matter if the poor sales were due to competition, weather, deliveries, quantities or pricing? What matters is that you have a line of defensive tactics that have been articulated and shelf ready for deployment to invigorate the forecasted sales over the next 3 to 4 weeks which are critical. The goal and focus must always be on the ability to quickly recover enough of your immediate revenue shortfall without *kicking the can* down the road. Project your revenue recovery prudently; break it up into a 60/40 quadrant where 35% of the loss will be made up here, 25% here, 25% here and the remaining 15% here. This becomes a believable course of action with the ability to adjust your ratios accordingly. Knowing the cause of certain stimulus will **not** give you the ability to keep them from happening again in the future. Your focus and energies have to be directed towards the proper reaction to issues and not to emphasis on their cause.

Many people confuse the proactive nature of business preparedness with the ability to preempt a situation. There are plenty of proactive, or defensive positions to be taken in an organization to mitigate risk. But the principles around mitigation of risk are most often tangible, and have a high probability of being identified. Such as theft, egregious accounting errors or transposed data entries. Few forecasts have been successful in identifying the fact that the competition's holiday pricing or promotional impacts on your share of wallet in the marketplace on yesterday's Black Friday were going to be "X". The speeds at which changes can and are being deployed by your competition prohibit meaningful immediate counter reactions in many situations, thus your need for a post promotional strategy agenda is imperative.

Now that your initial evaluation has determined the appropriate *How, Who and When,* you can begin **_examining_** your short term and long-term options. Here you will want to be decisive as to what your resolution will be, and the team or teams that will get it done.

We will introduce the following (3) step process to correct the current issue of late merchandise deliveries and lay the proceeding foundation procedures that will provide a process flow counter response to the issue long term.

You are then just a short hop away from your newfound zone of comfort. To ensure buy-in and recognize the functionality towards the achievements in your plan, you should create and publicize a time and action calendar for all to follow. This allows you and your team to **_execute_** the plans and illustrate deviations when necessary and most importantly, what your counter strategy will be.

All issues are NOT created equally and thus must follow a hierarchy for resolution. By readying yourself as a resolutionist and not a reactionist you will be the *go-to* person to devise a plan, assign a timeline and track the progress to resolve. You will quickly recognize the need to refocus your efforts and thus strengthen your natural ability to ward off the everyday negative rigors of life's issues that do not add value or credence to your existence.

In essence, you become your own enabler to replace your contentious, heart pounding worrisome moments for those that are more lighthearted, endorphin-releasing situations allowing for an enjoyable existence in business, relationships and life itself. As you begin your journey from where you are, to where you wish to be; you will better recognize those in your life who rely on others to acquire health, wealth and the most basic needs to sustain and enjoy life. These individual have found that the last few years have been extremely stressful and lacking emotional fulfillment. When times get tough, the shallow retreat inward and tend to keep to themselves. Thus starving those who have come to rely on them for direction, guidance and emotional nourishment. Whereas the strong reach out and deploy efforts to combine forces and strategies to prevail over these short-term issues.

There is a constant barrage of negative news stories; friends and family members losing their jobs, and general despair from just about everywhere you turn. You have to take these times for what they will soon become; history. Do not continue to dwell on these points for long. Take (15) minutes to rationalize the reasons and the issues from which they have occurred into account, and then look forward.

When it comes right down to it neither you, nor me, nor even Barack Obama, the current president of the United States can change the past or the present economical and emotional times. However, *your* future is yet to be molded by *your* hands. Your personal, financial and emotional well-being is yet to be directed and navigated by *your* actions.

One of my close personal friends, who happened to be a previous commander and chief at a retail establishment, and I became active members in our Social Media about the same time. We joined LinkedIn, Facebook, Twitter and all the social media sites. Amongst our many emails and tweets we exchanged, which were constantly filled with encouragement, evaluations of the economy and situation updates; I sent him this statement as a salutation:

Each day we are that much closer to getting back in the game, here's to a speedy tomorrow!

He wrote me back the following afternoon to let me know that he had placed those words on his desktop for inspiration... that made my day and soon thereafter he indeed was back in the game! You never know how something you do or say will affect others; it behooves you to make every effort to bring positive attributes to your game, as they are sure to be reciprocated.

The basic philosophies of happiness have not changed, if anything they are yearned more now than ever in most recent history by the majority of the population. We cannot allow these times to define who we are as a person. Remember to positively reach out as often as you can to a friend, loved one and yes, sometimes a stranger. You will reap the immediate reward personally and the later reward will come when you least expect it. We are the commanders of our *future* and not our past.

As this relates to retail, there is a bounty of positive emotional and financial treasures awaiting those who are able to recognize and react to a harmonious shopping community; who are demanding a more simplistic façade. *More* is no longer better and a multitude of choices are no longer as appealing. People are not interested in the quantity of products; they are interested in how the acquisition of obtaining the products made them feel. That is what will be remembered, simple, fair and enjoyable. Although we all immensely enjoy the ability to Google almost anything we can conceive, for many it has only served to quadruple the amount of questions they now have. What was once a *nice to know* just a few short years ago, has transformed into a *need to know* adding complexity to the decision making process.

Analysts inform us that a simple purchase decision made just a few short years ago that was done mostly from a need or want, now has transmuted into layers of online research and complex evaluations. The customer loyalty that business establishments once treasured and nurtured from their patrons has also become almost nonexistent. Consumer's loyalty has shifted from a particular store, to the place that has the lowest price offered at the time of their purchase decision. Convenience and service assumptions gathered through online comparisons and blogs follow closely behind this new decision making process. The successful retailers of the future will become an expert at intercepting the consumer's dynamic thought patterns.

They will accomplish greater success by adapting to change and exponentially smoothing the dynamics of pricing. All the while they will modernize their supply chain activities in tandem with their financially sound inventory to cash optimization cycles….

...But are the complexities that we assume necessary to quarantine a mistake real; is there something to be gained by chasing our past conditions with more robust technology and the exemplified stochastic calculations, which are by definition...assumptions laden with hypothesis? Perhaps the outcome wasn't because of a mistake, maybe... just maybe it's time for a more focused approach on where we're going as opposed to where we've been...and we'll call it;

THE NEW NORMAL?

Chapter 5

Retail Rules Of Engagement

What are the new rules???

As the consumers continue to evaluate and accept the conditions of our new economy, the retailers will continue to jockey for their share of wallet or simply put; the consumer's business. I recently have witnessed a communal theme that has begun to emerge in the retail and manufacturing sectors. Many of them seem to have found themselves, like deer in a headlight, caught in the shadows of yesteryear's Standard Operating Procedures and waiting to go back to business as usual.

Their impression of taking advantage of today's situation is to fortify their associate coffers and succession benches with what I call extreme talent at discounted prices. Part of this country's more opportunistic condition currently being deemed as the under employed. What some companies are failing to realize is that great associates alone do not great companies make.

When you begin to aggregate talent for the sake of having talent, and you do not focus on the person you're hiring with emphasis on their value to the team, anarchy will soon follow. It's like employing a group of musicians into your band without recognizing the integration of the instruments they play or the level of harmony they bring to your existing members. The successful companies will find and employee adaptive personnel who have their focus on responsive change, and the management of interactive communications with associates, consumers and vendors. They play many instruments, can harmonize with just about everyone and have a passion to lead the teams to victory. Average cost? $200k. Return on investment? *Priceless.*

Success will be commonplace for those organizations that strive to create space for true leadership that can inspire people to take calculated risks along with responsibility. When the company's focus has manifested from the quantity of highly qualified people to the high quality of people and that their accountability is rewarded, profitable growth to the organization is a by-product. For as many years as there has been a retail community, there have been those who have lead by *familiarity* and a *tribal knowledge* rather than by objectives and consumer centric demands. Leading by familiarity causes a lethargic belief that what they have learned in the past, will take them into the future;

...this is how we've always run the business...

What was good enough for their predecessors will be good enough for them and their successors. Ten to fifteen years ago this was a common way to keep your company rolling and respected by a loyal consumer group. People enjoyed the security of conforming to the same old dull routine day in and day out. It was predictable, you were comfortable and everyone was acquiescent. What happened within the personal and daily lives of the team members in their homes was generally fodder for their business lives.

But oh how things have changed!

Today you have to incorporate an aspect of visionary principles when deducing a resolution to an issue. What worked just a few short years ago is lost in today's environment and if you aren't careful, can quickly become irrelevant tomorrow. For example, take the premise of the use of historical standards that many current retail sales and service level analysis are based on today. Even with the facts as we know them today, many organizations evaluate effectiveness and their operating positions based on historical patterns of a similar period last year.

When you use these ideologies as your gauge of trajectory as opposed to a basic relational foundation, you begin the practice of mining for what I call fool's gold. Your registered value points depicting the differentiation on your business last year or the year before have long since been silenced. The last eight to thirteen weeks, at most, have the key to your successful predictions of the future and a relevant forecast capability. Just the introduction of technology here isn't the answer. Even the most powerful data mining equipment, four-tier technology and quantum mathematical systems will only produce the debauched forecasts of last year's business. Without steering and proper guidance, like your car, the systems can get you to the wrong place quicker.

So who are these leaders that continue to proliferate the organizations with these ancient adaptations of the truth? You will recognize the *familiarity business leaders* from their focus to base future goals on annualized historical accomplishments. They rally over a statistic that shows an improvement over last year, when last year may just as well have been *horrific* to the year before. Thus leaving you flat to two years ago performance when costs have risen 45% since then. This Neanderthal basis for communicating the statistics has a premise that ensures confusion and suppression of ideas and advanced thinking.

You can easily identify these leaders as those who aren't willing to spend a dime on systems or personnel to save a dollar. In Latin we call these leaders; *Homacous **Nickle&Dime**leostatus Eraticatus...* I believe that is their scientific retail name, I may be wrong so don't quote me on this one. *–just having some fun- do not look those words up-*.

To this very day, some believe that there are yet some *missing links* and descendants of this make-believe tribe that still exist in corporate leadership. Tribal knowledge is defined as; *those inherited rules and disciplines that are neither documented nor tested for today's retail environment, but are religiously adhered to by the ancient leaders and their respective disciples.* In my research, I have found that there are still quite a few divisions that are being governed by such a Jurassic thought process executive.

The keepers of this knowledge can, and often do illustrate case study after case study of those corporate entities that have purchased new technology and failed shortly thereafter. They typically make this revelation for self-preservation as well as an inability to handle or govern change. For every one company that has deployed cutting edge technology and failed, eight have succeeded. The relevant difference is the use of consultants and experienced, open-minded executive decision makers. **In retail, you either change or someone else will do it for you!**

Today's organizations, and those who will be here tomorrow are striving harder now than ever before to differentiate themselves from their competition. For that very reason, someone who has a familiar background and a history of running a similar type of business as yours, may not have what it takes to manage your emerging *new* business goals. Retail is a dynamic beast; that which worked for you yesteryear has already been duplicated, and in some cases, refined and honed by your competition to a level better than yours. You must be innovative and motivated to become the best or suffer the ramifications therein.

Executive leaders must understand and commit themselves to a mantra that encompasses the following doctrine;

> *"in order to succeed in today's hostile sales and profit environment, you must first learn and understand your challenges and obstacles from those who carry the load daily; then create a symbiotic relationship with your people and processes to embrace those challenges and remove the obstacles with attuned technology".*
> *Rlt 2011*

The process of retail is a simple methodology; however most have found it extremely difficult to have the right goods, in the right store, at the right price, at the right time with any consistent cadence. This occurs most often when the true consumer response factors are overlooked or called *red* when they are clearly *blue*.

An example of this would be that company (ABC) has a predetermined reactive group of business rules based on the **_red_** condition. These are high tech, laser guided, pinpoint accurate processes from new margin sensitive indices that are automatically applied to replenishment and distribution systems; optimal pricing strategies deployed to competition enriched demographics and accelerated promotional strategies are planned to increase turn and minimize markdowns. That would truly be a respectful series of responses, costly in both time and resources, but respectful. However, had the company deployed the business intelligence models along with professional accountability processes in practice today, they would have revealed the issue for what it truly was; **_blue_**.

"Utilizing a series of phone calls to the store operation personnel, it is ascertained that an offensive manufacturing mistake on the packaging labels caused consumer outrage in several stores. Head of Store Operations decreed that the merchandise be uniformly removed from the sales floor in all stores immediately awaiting disposition...but for some reason, the merchants were not contacted."

Consumers, for many retailers are becoming an endangered species. Retailers must regroup and take calculated and measurable steps to ensure their survival and ability to flourish during this dynamic transition. Much like many species in nature, retailers and their customers share a symbiotic relationship that when nurtured appropriately, both enjoy a mutual existence. But if the consumer feels shunned, they quickly adapt to similar offerings from your competitors and you perish.

It is no secret that many companies have recently made what initially appeared to be a good technological or marketing investments, to change who they <u>are</u>. Only to later find they lost their identity, hence brand, and ultimately their consumer who was loyal to who they <u>were</u>.

Once Upon A Time

When retail was in its infancy, under guidance from the generals; Mr. Woolworth, Mr. Kresge, Mr. Walton, and the likes, the formula was much easier to comprehend and execute. The market share was confined to the radius by which your customers were willing to drive to their local store. Up until the late 90's and early part of the new millennium you, as a retailer, enjoyed a captured market and could dictate the consumer's likes and dislikes by the amount of inventory you stacked in their faces and what color starburst-pricing banner you utilized to lure them to purchase.

In today's retail environment, the process is no longer a simple one, and your market share is guided by your ability to attract and retain your core consumers, while attracting a constant flow of new ones. Egregious real estate growth, ubiquitous product and pricing strategies across dissimilar channels and time honored; out dated promotional practices took their toll on some of the best brands in the industry during 2006 - 2009. And yet, as retailers find themselves expanding departments, adding technology and reducing their store staff all in the name of retail utopia; the end is surely near for a selected group of such retailers. They have pushed the consumer to the brink of no return, and they are oblivious to the emotional impact caused by their short-sited decisions.

As I mentioned, the challenge is to simultaneously prospect for new customers, who have been left holding their wallets by all the closed companies they used to shop with, while you retain your core consumers. Without the right people, product, marketing, and supply chain strategies working symbiotically, you will soon find yourself at the bottom of the heap and struggling for survival.

There are unsubstantiated business models being decreed daily in retail that have competing or debilitating conditions. These mantras of certain death come from a variety of sources. Finance, Merchandising, Store Operations and even sometimes the President will campaign for one or more of these top five declarations for improvement listed:

A: Ubiquitous pricing for *all divisions at all times.*
B: Increased product service levels *across the board.*
C: GM% increase by 20 basis points in 6 months.
D: Markdown optimization. Period.
E: Increased Markups through Imports.

If one or more of the aforementioned improvement declarations hasn't yet confronted you, rest assured that it's coming as the retail evolutionary cycle continues. As you review the above, note that each of the conditions relies on one or more of the other conditions when evaluating sustainability in your market place. Contrary to some beliefs, you cannot have the same pricing in all stores and truly optimize your markdowns. You can however improve the efficiencies of your markdowns in a singular focused environment, but that's not true *optimization.*

Properly attuned business models rely heavily on the continual improvement of their mathematical relationship between the financial critical mass, technologies and eager capable personnel. The kinetic Rules of Retail have been, and always will be an easy ACT to follow when you have the right *actors* in place.

Accurately documented process of consistently buying consumer relevant merchandise for as little as possible;

Consistently selling said merchandise to an identified and nurtured consumer at a price as high as the market will bear;

Timely liquidation of nonperforming assets for no less than cost, or a derivative thereof along the way that supports you R.O.I. assumptions.

By following these simple but effective rules you will be laying the very foundation by which future goals can and will be achieved.

Now let's take a walk into the retail daily grind, shall we?

Chapter 6

The Daily Grind
(Part: 1 of 3)

I t's 8 a.m. on a Monday morning and Norman Baulker is frantically gathering his reports and information from last week's business. Suddenly Norman notices that his sales and stock status report, *which only happens to be the holy grail of data*, is not in his overflowing and tattered report bin.

"Oh please let this be a dream!" Norman utters to himself as he gently messages his temples as to restrict the onset of the inevitable migraine that erupts when he allows too much of the day's pressures to get to him.

This *managed* chaos is repeated each week, at this time, by a team of buyers, planners and analysts who are laser focused on preparing their contributions for THE 9:00 a.m. MANDATORY staff meeting. Each week Norman stresses over the same fears, as do all the merchants, and that is being asked a series of questions during the meeting for which you do not have an immediate, thought provoking, substantive answer.

Norman calls out, this time with just a flicker of disparity in his voice.

"Has anyone seen the SSR this morning?"

The silence was deafening.

Under normal circumstances and general office protocol, Norman's request would have been met with a parade of answers. Those answers would typically indicate everything from the last person seen with a copy of the report, to a known system delay announcement circulated by the technology team. However, on this occasion Norman commandeered silence. Not even a whisper, there were no muffled water cooler conversations, hurried footsteps, frantic keystrokes, aggressive coffee sipping...*NOTHING*!

Norman took his feet, briefly abandoning his frantic search through his fruitless; paper brimming bins that bowed under the weight of the *I'll get to it* reports, and made his way to the threshold of his office. There he slowly moved his chin down towards his chest and peered just over the black horizontal rim of his prescription reading glasses. He doesn't really need the glasses, but his wife...well that's a story for another day. The merchandise and buying area was an absolute ghost town. Not a single person in sight, and there was much to do, for goodness sakes; It's Monday!

Scratching his head, Norman turned and moved slowly back towards his desk. As he pondered the potential causes for desertion of the area, did I miss the fire alarm; was there a medical emergency; perhaps it's Sunday and I just imagined that people were here 20 minutes ago...

Just then, Norman glanced at his monitor to see a familiar email logo and animated happy face declaration on his monitor.

Norman took ahold of his mouse, guided the pointer over the red flagged email and double clicked the message. It was from Jamie Craoughton in human resources and it said:

"JOIN US FOR COFFEE & DOUGHNUTS!"

After reading the entry just below the announcement it became very apparent why *everyone* suddenly was interested in being in the same place at the same time:

"8:15 a.m. in the cafeteria this morning! We will announce the winners of the Red Cross Donation raffle!

WINNERS MUST BE PRESENT!"

"Well, there you go" Norman thought to himself.

"Why would anyone concern themselves about running a business when you can have free coffee, doughnuts and a chance to win a 55inch LED TV?"

Norman was more upset that it was now 8:53 a.m. and they clearly had already announced the winner of the T.V., then the fact that his comrades had left him. He envisioned that his name was called first in the raffle and because he was WORKING!!!! …Someone else was going to enjoy *his* television.

Norman Baulker is a well-groomed, average height, medium build senior buyer in his mid 40's for one of the highest ranking and most profitable categories in the company. Norman has an exceptional eye for picking product and an acute sense of quantum mathematics that he uses to balance his merchandise assortment. Working with his planner and allocation analyst, he is sensitive of the correlation between the purchase price and initial retail, quantity and receipt flow, promotional cadence and liquidation timing to reveal a highly acceptable gross margin return on investment. He's married with two kids and a dog. He enjoys getting the job done and heading home to his family at a respectable time. Unfortunately, that balance of life and work makes him a target for the *over-takers* in the office.

These are the young *hotshots* or *newbies* who have their career goals calibrated in their own little dynamic succession. According to their timelines, the process from entry level to a head position in merchandising should take somewhere between 6 and 18months. These radical retail youths morbidly resemble undertakers in society. And I have the utmost respect for undertakers. Their roles sometimes mean they aren't as upset with the *death of a career* as they may appear because it means additional business and advancement opportunities for them.

They are truly sorry for your job loss, but; *"could you leave the lamp and rug in your office?"* They just step over, on and around the bodies that happen to occupy the rungs of their ascent of the corporate ladder. They revel in the overtly loud and misguided conversations with others to illustrate their superficial relationship of time-spent versus value added to the corporation.

"I just got the vendor to take another five cents per unit off of my initial cost!" one of them yells.

If only they captured the true service level of the item, they would have noticed that this vendor has been short on 93% of the orders they've shipped the company since early 2010 and accounting has setup an automatic charge-back memo for their repeated violations.

This is what I deem as fluid knowledge, and should be applied consistently to your numbers for validation.

Upon seeing Norman shut down his computer, grab his jacket and turn off his lights, you hear an audible declaration from one of the over-takers that would emulate a yell to a friend at a crowded stadium:

"Goodnight Norman!", "Does your son have *ANOTHER* game tonight?"

Which is immediately followed by a more subdued, almost whisper for those closest to hear; *"must be nice".*

You know the type. Truth be told, if you could harness their somewhat religious efforts to dethrone their co-workers and focus that energy into a more productive ritual of analyzing data and resolving issues, retail utopia would not be far away.

The company has just come off of a very controversial and expensive two-week marketing campaign. Controversial; because this was not in the budget and to make it happen, vendor *offerings* were required. I call them offerings because it takes on an almost religious connotation. Picture if you will, all the vendors who do business with the company are aligned in pews based on the category of merchandise they sell to the organization.

Each buyer is required to call; or as they like to portray it, *send an offering plate down the pew for a contribution from each vendor*, and report to their divisional merchandise manager what they *took up during service*. After a few prayers and a *come to Jesus* speech from the vice president of merchandise, enough money to initiate the campaign is accumulated from the vendors in a few weeks.

The president will usually send a note of gratitude to the participating vendors and thank them for being *team players*. These offerings will -by the way- be recouped by the vendors on the next round of price negotiations for product. It is just a redundant cycle of stealing from Peter to pay Paul, but it is what it is.

Norman was in concert with his peers in the marketing meeting last month proclaiming,

"The sale misses over the last month and a half were due to a lack of customer traffic."

A parade of agreement nods began and ended right on cue like the synchronized penguins in that wonderful adaptation with Morgan Freeman as narrator.

This proclamation seemed reasonable at the time because frankly, unless customers are coming into the stores, you can't sell your merchandise. You need a catalyst for the customers to respond.... and there's no better way than a good ole' fashioned in your face: *SALE!*

NOW WHAT?

Norman's expectations are that he will have surpassed his sales plan, as the early global marketing indications were very positive.   Or *where* there early global marketing indicators?

You be the judge.... here's how it went down.

"Hey, I just got a call from store #1621," said one of the *newbies* in the allocation pit.

The allocation pit, as it is lovingly called, is the area created by *(24)* parallel cubicles in the office that run perpendicular to the buying and planning offices in the merchandising neighborhood.

Like prairie dogs trying to get a peak at impending danger, heads begin to poke above the cubicles to get a listen. She continues her story

"and the manager said they have a line of customers waiting for their store to open this morning with the sales brochure in their hands!!"

With wide eyes, toothy grins and pent up demand for irrational exuberance; no one took the time to assess that this was just one occurrence from one person, and unquantifiable.

Who among this group will stand up and announce;

"Wait a minute! Isn't it too early to read this data as a trend?"

…Anyone…. anyone?

Of course not! Nobody wants to be the *deflator* or *doomsayer* under such a euphoric occasion. Why that person would surely be deemed as someone who wasn't good for the team; and with such a branding would be delivered to the *over-takers* on a silver platter to suffer their wrath.

And that my friend is how a simple statement becomes gospel and is commandeered as the official measurement of a marketing campaign. All of their hopes and aspirations for a successful sales campaign are predicated on *one* phone call from *one* manager about an *unquantifiable* event.

Just like the secret you told the person to your immediate left at the conference and that person reciprocated your secret to the person next to them and so on and so on. As the words travel and time goes by, unintended enhancements are added, the story changes, becomes something of a joke gone horribly bad. Try as they might the human element intervenes and emotion overcomes the pursuit of facts; and in no time flat a fable is born.

By the end of the day, that one response grew into a six o'clock parking lot yell from one of Norman's peers,

"Hey, did you hear that the sale has been so successful that the stores have had to hire extra security to manage the lines that wrap for blocks?" Norman could only smile and with one arm raised in a waving gesture, dissolves his body into his car and heads home.

Don't you just marvel over the power of half-truths and wishful thinking?

The Daydream

"Please reveal to me that I have at least beaten last year's sales numbers!"

This is Norman's silent prayer to the *Retail Gods* as he begins to fantasize into a daydream about being *pointed* to, and heroically called out for a job well done in the meeting….

*****

The room is silent; all eyes are on the documents before them.   The assistants have meticulously arranged the reports in a hierarchical order some (15) minutes before the meeting began.   Executives – full package of (45) pages, Vice Presidents – (32) pages, the (13) pages of corporate overhead and bottom line impact analysis removed, Directors average (18) pages and all others get a (6) page synopsis covering their areas of responsibility.

The head of merchandising leaps to their feet; looks up at the ceiling and then down to me. I, without expression, act as if I don't notice the extended finger from their hatchet chop motion arm towards me.

*"this man...oh...**this man**!!!   He is the only one to have beaten **all** the sacred factors; revenue, margin rate, margin dollars and unit growth by (40%) or more."* Exclaims the senior vice president of merchandising. Norm shrugs his shoulders and exposes the palms of his hands as he half cocks his head to one side and says; *" I only planned* for 25%." With that, he bows his head in guiltless shame to a round of thunderous applause.

...and...scene...
*****

The fact of the matter is; very little accolades are distributed at those meetings. The majority of the meetings are those heart-wrenching ones where one of Norman's colleagues gets their head handed to them for missing their plan by (10%).

It was just at last Monday's meeting that Norman cringed as the passive aggressive children's wear buyer attempted to justify their 90% of plan results as a positive step in the right direction. She was quick to acknowledge the fact that the tough economic conditions have relinquished most other areas to much less desirable results.

Norman felt her pain as he began to hear that deep, polished voice respond;

"How 'bout I pay you (10) % less this week? Oh NOW that (90) % accuracy rate you're so proud of begins to register doesn't it missy?"

That's Mr. Trent, a military groomed; school of hard knocks summa cum laude; and a proverbial PhD in retail. He is the Executive Vice President of Supply Chain Management, but if the truth be known, not much happens in the company without his approval and authority. If he weren't so brilliant, he'd make you sick. But most of the time his predictions are spot on, and when he's wrong; well, everyone learns a valuable lesson in applied economics and consumer centric demand patterns. Oh, and I would be remised if I didn't mention the importance of properly adjusting the historical dynamic linear regression merchandise models in a timely manner.

His favorite statement:

"If you listen, learning becomes a by-product."

WISHING FOR MORE!!

If the business could be won or lost on hope then Norman has a fighting chance. Norman has been here many times before, compiling data and searching for the truth. His hopes are simple ones; he simply wishes that for a change he would get an opportunity to bask in well-deserved lofty sales gains. But not your typical one-sided sales gains, Norman longed for the kind of sales gains that are accompanied by a healthy profit margin.

Low and behold; just as he begins to digest the initial data and produce his synopsis, his nemesis, Mike Thompson eclipses the doorway to Norman's office, chest out, Cheshire cat grin:

"Blew the plan *OUT* of the *WATER!*"

Exclaims the *one who should just die….* at least that's what the merchandise team associates say in the hallway just after he struts by them.

Mike is 6'5", athletically built, early 30's, single and has a remarkable talent of making just about everyone around him painfully aware of their inadequacies.

Every morning around 8:45 a.m. as Mike enters the building, the merchandise associates in unison have the same reaction. Their chins down, semi-bowing bodies are magnetized along the walls as he aristocratically delivers his patented, *and by any account, flipped –* salutation. With his eyes half closed; he spastically jerks his head up as in a half-nod of the head to everyone under the rank of Vice President. It is the lack of respect conveyed to them and his *holier than thou* attitude that warrants a wish for death in their minds.

Now perched on tippy toes in Norman's threshold, right and left arms raised above his head in a basketball shooting stance. Mike announces in a loud obnoxious voice;

"...two seconds on the clock, Thompson shoots...SCORE!!!..."

Because he is so self-centered, Mike clearly refuses to acknowledge Norman's non-emotional pursuit of his own truth in the numbers. After several more annoying and ritualistic phrases from Mike, Norman has no choice but to retort indignantly without looking away from his monitor,

"I'm working on my numbers right now Mike."

Mike, who does not feel in the least bit offended by the statement gets the message, not from what Norman said; but how he said it; and continues his *march of arrogance* away from Norman's office. He moves down the hall five steps and although Norman tries not to; he hears the *"blew the plan OUT of the WATER!"* six more times until the hall runs out of offices or people close enough to be engulfed by Mike's irritating and indignant mantra. But, in reality, it is mostly jealously Norman feels, green eyed, I'll be damned...*jealousy.*

Norman breathes a sigh of relief having concluded his data gathering excursion and Microsoft Excel model input. A few years ago Norman joined the masses in complaining that a $2 billion dollar a year company should not be using Excel as a means of data gathering and reporting, but the chant fell on deaf, and shall I say it, **dumb** ears.

So the inexpensive process of gathering, entering and double-checking the numbers takes about 2 hours per person for the 27 people who perform this ritual each week. With relative salaries in mind, that comes to a little over $80,000 eighty thousand dollars a year in productivity. Not to mention the inaccuracy and lack of analysis completed on the data. Eighty percent of the time was utilized gathering the information and twenty percent was used to make million dollar business decisions.

How inexpensive is it again?

Unfortunately for Norman, hope wasn't enough today; his numbers aren't quite as good as he had anticipated. After entering his statistics in the preformatted and executive approved Excel templates, what he finds is the fact that he sold the same average weekly number of units during the promotion as he did during a non-promotional week, just at a lesser retail; which delivered a sub par profit margin.

What went wrong? Norman begins to forecast the battery of questions that await him in a few moments at the coveted Monday morning status meeting. Did we not advertise the right items for this time of year? Was our pricing strategy in line with our competition? Were the stores prepared to handle this intense untested marketing campaign? Did the allocations area use the wrong historical basis to allocate the merchandise and thus missed the proposed promotional store distribution targets? Had Norman known any of the answers to these questions prior to running the promotion; what would he have done differently? …. and equally as important, what will his next move be to correct the damage and solidify a process that won't repeat this performance in the future?

Chapter 7

Creating Value / Accounting For Change

To reinvent your organization's functionality and relational requirements to create a promising value proposition is challenging enough. To do it while recognizing system impact, results on the capitalized investments and human resource needs is something entirely different. Although you will find many case studies on the subject, you will rarely find one that is appropriate for your particular situation. To mitigate risks you will want to utilize the following three-part process I describe below as the **ARC** of retail prior to engaging your restructuring or rebuilding efforts.

One of the most important questions to answer that has yet to gain traction in organizations that are engaged in change today is; will our efforts result in creating value for our consumers? This typically occurs because most organized efforts towards change rely on the quantitative aspect of the definition of change and not the qualitative and emotional impacts. It really isn't difficult to measure the variance in a group of hypotheses that relate to the cost, time or space of a product offering. The difficult and more important factor is one that answers the questions related to the consumer's experience, needs, wants and above all; how much will your customer VALUE your change?

There are as many diverse concepts and approaches to creating value in retail as there are retailers today. The most common of these approaches used in the past couple of years, Supply Chain Management, has seen little to no results after many frustrating hours of implementation and budget busting software installations. The efficiency models that are sought after are rarely calibrated for the company that is exploring them and the strategies are often an afterthought. When properly managed, an executive leader in the company that clearly has the process, financial and operational comprehension of the organization generally heads this model successfully. The Supply Chain is typically the lowest common denominator on this headline challenge to create value and the frequency by which the operational course will change can be stunning for some. That's why you cannot make this area a training ground for the new associates, nor can it be a change agent for someone from another branch of the organization.

Why does the course change so often? I can answer that question for you with two words: *Consumer sentiment.* Because the efficiency model is not regulated by the personal and flexible needs and wants of the controlling public, the adjustments are far more frequent in occurrence, than is optimal by nature. The gap generally occurs when the organization fails to capitalize on the function of centralizing the common key areas of supply chain. This can be achieved while the essence of individualization within the business units is preserved. Strategies are the key enabler when adopting technology to your project for creating value and ensuring that the rational business changes are accounted for.

No doubts that the innovations over these last few years have been substantial in the realm of project management. But can you fully claim a dominant factor of usage on what you currently have? Each new introduction of technology has been done so on the premise of faster, smarter, better; but has your organization's leadership, guidance and ability to harness such power been elevated accordingly? When the dust settles from our current economic situation, will your team posses the right tools, under the right strategies with a focus on centralization? Or will you require the expertise from outside to ensure consistency of your message to your consumers, and the control of assets throughout your supply chain?

The A.R.C. of Retail

Executives in retail, in an effort to command and absorb a lager share of the consumer's wallet, are refining their assessment of the more traditional competitive approach to their business. The organizations that are able to successfully manage the leap from *good to great* are adapting to a more simplified process of decision-making that applies the **A.R.C.** of retail.

The **ARC** bridges the gap between robotic decision-making and proper compelling thoughts and laser-focused execution that creates leaders, not dictators. This principle's very existence relies on the business hypothesis that uniformity exists through a correlation of **A**ccountability, **R**esponsibility and **C**apability. The ARC utilizes a simple approach that measures competence and ability based on a foundation of practicality. The success of the project is weighted by measuring the degree by which the ARC is assigned.

When I approach a company and begin my thesis on where they've been so that I can deliver a comprehensive roadmap for the where they want to be, I enroll these practices that require full disclosure. The majority of reasons for project or initiative failures in the past have been easily identified when you triangulate the objectives using this ARC methodology.

- Was the person(s) held <u>A</u>ccountable for {*developing*} <u>and</u> {*deploying*} the process to meet the expectations?
  - o *Or were they given a task to accomplish with some rudimentary guidelines?*

- Were they given total <u>R</u>esponsibility to assess, construct and determine the outcome and timeline?
  - o *Or did someone apply a deadline and rules around do's and don'ts for the project?*

- And lastly, were they <u>C</u>apable of bringing the project to a successful conclusion?
  - o *Or were expectations set which would conclude with a touchdown given to the pitcher of the basketball team?*

Were the *right* people assigned to the *right* job based on the strategic objective and for the *right* reasons?

To reach your goals, be sure that the basis assigns all (3) A.R.C. complements in accord to the task with clearly defined objectives and expected results listed within the subject matter;

1. Accountability: Full unwavering authorization to make decisions and change course if necessary. This is a commitment to accept the vision and fulfill your requirements, in short: you willingly or have an obligation to accept the responsibility.

2. Responsibility: The epitome of accepting all outcomes after endorsing and providing or receiving directional clarity of the objectives. This is an endorsement to take the blame, and spread the fame.

3. Capability of making decisions based on accurate information, training to do what's right, process to close end to end issues.

Here is something that may help you remember and properly apply this principle to your projects:

The team, which was held accountable *for their respective parts, is praised for surpassing the predicted outcome. Their leader was* responsible *for ensuring that based on the team's requests; they had all the tools and information necessary to make and execute decisions. An assessment of the team's members was conducted pre-launch and concluded with a 92% factor, which affirmed that the team was* capable *of accomplishing their objectives effectively and efficiently.*

Without this **ARC**, there is no bridge to success!

Positioning your company to do the very best requires ***one;*** who not only understands your business model, but also your business needs. My aforementioned statement is not a misnomer, when I stated **one**, I do indeed imply that one person must be in charge of the final decision-making process. Without this one stopping point, your organization's efforts and benefits will be diminished immensely.

What a lot of companies have found is that when you try to improve business by means of *consensus*, you end up with *chaos*. The process does not start off that way; most companies truly do believe that more heads are better than one. What has generally failed is the illusive consensus based on the big picture. Each area has their individual strengths, knowledge and capability. However they rarely breach outside of their immediate areas to see or recognize the supply chain impact.

To realize that just like the individual colors of the painter's pallet; each associate brings to the table a very unique set of skills. Those skills alone do not ensure that the business will produce an outcome as good as that of a true artist's rendition. So when you have the respective heads of departments come together; a governor of such needs to be appointed that can efficiently and effectively utilize each person's strengths, identifies their weaknesses and configures the team for optimized results. Certainly one could argue that Rembrandt produced some truly magnificent work; my challenge would be that his art, which appeals to a large populace, has one creator. There are very few people who can duplicate that work. Unless you are truly gifted with an eye for art, your ability to comprehend, identify and recreate such art goes without saying.

Such is the same in business. Having a team produce consistently good, well-organized work depends greatly on the individual in charge. The individual has to be a great coach, not a director, his team has to <u>want </u>to succeed and feel empowered to achieve their goals without constant intervention or direction.

Listen To The Statistics

Respectfully, capital gains in business have a mathematical purity that requires less of an artistic eye. It has a dimension that follows more principle objectives and a focus on forecasting and planning. It demands that the individuals act in accordance with their teams with a mutual ***respect*** of the numbers, but always ***obey*** the analysis. *Analyze twice and execute once....* I always say.

On any given day a retailer's worst nightmare coincides with their wildest dream. Customers come to shop! Your marketing and advertising achieved the goal of increased footsteps! Now comes the double-edged sword? The assortment offerings, and more precise, the balance therein have not been forecasted properly; or not at all and you leave tons of money on the table. Not to mention disappointed and boisterous consumers in the wake. When you are selling merchandise, you must never diminish the fact that you're fueling the engine called PROFITS. This particularly ravenous engine relies on a precise balance of gasoline=revenue and oxygen=gross margin to maintain solvency and to continue running smooth for years to come.

If the mixture is not balanced to the needs of the engine, over time the engine will shut down....or will *be* shut down, possibly by another driver, whose sole purpose will be to alleviate the toxic spewing of cash reserves into the atmosphere caused by your neglect. Either a board of directors in a public company, or executive powers in a private institution will make the decision to; shut it down!

A litany of legal wrangling then pursues with a nomination of the proper heads to roll and an appointed sergeant of arms to carryout the declaration. The company is then infused with *masters of mayhem* and highly organized dismantling experts that take about (90 - 180) days to erase the issue and your existence from the retail and business landscape.

These *mechanics*, as we will refer to them, are not an abomination of business salvation as they are commonly referred. They are true opportunist and are highly skilled and efficient at getting the job done. The mechanics I am referring to are a division of much larger foundations known as Asset Recovery operations; those of us in retail call them Liquidators. The growth and prosperity enjoyed by the liquidators are a symbiotic evolution from our *free wheeling* retail mavericks from the late 90's and early 2000's.

Perfectly good retail operations were being abandoned for the sellable value of their parts. The liquidators relied on a very simple formula to take a struggling retailer, whose business continued to decline precipitously in the last few years, and create a sales boom. They perfected a means to show the consumer exceptional value, with a sense of urgency attached, and their mousetrap would forsake all others.

And after trials and tribulations they settled on the initialism; G.O.B., **G**oing **O**ut of **B**usiness. These three letters became the means to create chum in the sea of blissfully quiet retail shoppers.   The mantra for the liquidators became...*If you sign it, they will come!*

This worked so well that it became a focused target of the state attorney general's offices concerned for the publics' inability to stop themselves from spending their last dollar when prompted by this ingenious ploy.

How/why did so many retailers capsize their vessels in those defining hours of the economic hurricane in the later part of 2008 and early 2009? A lot of the answers can be found by reviewing the solitary actions of the captains of these enterprises who unknowingly precipitated controlled chaos.

Retail executives found solace in their ability to grow top line revenues, without the coordinated efforts of a solid foundation of personnel and technologies to support these top-heavy efforts and control expenses. Pirates of profits, I called them. Every industry had them, and retail was no exception. These were the self-loathing leaders who put their current share price, driven solely by top line revenues, in lockstep with their own miserable self-worth.

These barons of the abominable committed their followers to a short-lived euphoria of rapid comp store sales growth and unbridled costly store expansion. All of this while bellowing *Geronimo* as they gripped the release cords of their Golden Parachutes as they leapt from their Hindenburg.

Their antics resembled that of a drunken pillage of the commercial real estate venue and the raping of product gross margins. It was during these times where even the most hideous of retail occupancy space, as long as it was in a Life-Style Center, were submitted with a pro forma that resembled Treasure Island's bounty. And thus, commanded an unsustainable long-term revenue generating, margin poor promotional cadence to offset the absurd lease expenses.

Consumers are demanding value in their shopping experience. No longer was it enough to have quantity or depth in a particular commodity; there must be an intrinsic value proposition that is easily understood and so compelling that purchase logic takes a back seat. A good example of this retail premise used successfully by some key retailers is the **multiple unit logic expression**, or m.u.l.e. This dynamic / simplistic process can be used to compel the average consumer to fill their shopping basket on command. It places the commodity into an easily recognized value as in the case of {10 for $10} or {2 for $20}. These *mules* have the ability to carry the consumer from the shopping isles to the register without even breaking a *promotional* sweat.

Creating value is academic, accounting for change needs to be endemic, and the consequences can be unmerciful.

If you truly listen, learning becomes a by-product.

Chapter 8

Understanding Risk

Since the beginning of time we have been basically programmed to avoid risk. The perception that a person could benefit from a certain amount of risk has been controversial to say the least. And to be perfectly frank, the topic of risk under today's circumstances is not a very popular topic. Society has conditioned our focus on steering way clear of risk, which is the relevant fear of saying, or doing something that may cause an undesirable outcome. Most people will tell you to steer clear of risky situations rather than the effective process of risk mitigation, which reduces the probability of an undesirable outcome.

However, risk management will always be somewhat of a controversy because the realm of exactness does not exist when you are dealing with human desires and emotions. And lets face the facts, the very concept of retail in general, places you and your corporation's products right in the epicenter of human wants, needs, desires and emotions. For this reason you really have no recourse, you must entertain the process of risk management and the capital investments needed to sustain a balance between reaching for more; and pulling back when the risk is too high.

Now you are relegated to the unenviable task of answering the proverbial questions. How high is high? When is enough, enough? The two most extreme groups of leadership, the fearless and the failures have pondered these and many similar questions over the years. Each segment will tell you that they had good reasons for their decisions and each would be correct. When one group believes that they **can't** achieve their goals because the risk is too great; and the other believes that they **will** achieve their goals because they are taking risks...they both are likely to reach their destinations.

With today's volatile pendulum swings from irrational exuberance to outright panic in the retail sector, the third most valuable asset great corporations can have is *knowledge*. Having a well-trained knowledgeable staff can greatly enhance your ability to capitalize on risks. You may have heard of the "risk to reward ratio" which is a rudimentary equation that measures the amount of risk involved to the amount of reward obtained upon a conclusion. The theory illustrates that the greater the risk, the greater the reward. The harmony comes from the balance of the two. Gamblers often times forget that the house has the overwhelming odds in their favor and fail to mitigate their risk while eyeing the reward as they roll the dice.

I have found that the most beneficial type of knowledge that is congenial with risk is one that I deem *fluid knowledge*. Not the type of knowledge that is garnered through years of specific education, computational math, or sophisticated technological program languages or even the relative retail experiences of the past. No, the best knowledge is exemplified by the fact that it transcends all the aforementioned characteristics and pivots on practicality, economics and speed. As you get to know me you will realize that I will rarely put a statement out there for interpretation, I will attempt to back my thesis up with some common everyday knowledge.

The reason I feel that "fluid knowledge" is the new standard of thought generation for out times is that change happens quickly and to stay relevant, you have to think differently. For instance, at our current growth rate of doubling every two years in technology and information sharing, we will render that which was learned in 2010 obsolete by 2013. Before you shake this little fact off as rhetoric, think about the technology you used around work and at home just 5 years ago. Most of that same technology is outdated or obsolete today. Now apply the exponential growth factor of 2.5 – 3.0 to the next few years going forward and you see my point for fluid knowledge.

The risks, as well as their root causes, will be different for you and your company in the coming years. That which you are learning today will not get you past the obstacles of a foreseeable tomorrow. We have yet to be faced with some of the obstacles of tomorrow, but they will come…they always come. Change is happening and you will want to embrace those who recognize and have adapted to the facts. There are a few who know the impact of the fact that Japan is currently pushing 14 trillion bits per second through a single strand of optic cable fiber. To give you a reference of the amount of data, that is equivalent to approximately 210 million phone calls every second. When that much information is capable of being disseminated to your consumers that fast, you have to be poised to make changes rapidly and succinctly with your financial acumen in check.

Identifying individuals with this unique quality usually means that you have recognized on your own, or employed a consulting expert to evaluate your specific needs. These needs would include;

- Recognizing the most prevalent risks you will face.
- What external factors will be driving those risks?
- Who will facilitate the management of these risks?

Risk has developed into a (4) four-letter word in the retail vernacular. Although the proper placement of well-poised risk is essential to growth and profits, it has been overused and managed poorly.

The main reason for this is that the overwhelming majority of executives are suppressors of risk. They wish to identify; corral and mitigate it rather than categorize, measure and manage the outcome for the rewards endowed within. The self-preservationist practice of averting risk by your key decision makers' is not only unhealthy for your business, it consistently breeds' mediocrity. It accomplishes this by establishing a *bunt* mentality from their major league associates; who have the ability and passion to *knock it out of the park*.

To identify if you are amongst these oppressive coaches, you have to answer the following questions.

1. Has your company identified and illustrated to all associates the risk factors to achieving the top 3 objectives for the year?

2.   Have you witnessed a time when an excuse for the sales miss was related to the weather and then a compelling scenario is illustrated on how the loss will be made up?

3.   85% or more of your executive team have weekly meetings with a group of (15) or less associates under their jurisdiction. Sometimes referred to as "fireside chats".

If your answer to all (3) questions was No; there is a strong probability that your executive team is more risk adverse and thus have potential to stifle the company's talent and everyone's opportunities to succeed.

You see risk and greed are first cousins in the world of retail as well as life in general. From the words of the great "Gordon Gekko" in the movie "Wall Street"; *"greed is good".*[2]

With that, one could assess that *risk* therefore can't be all that bad, and your assumption would be correct. In life and retail, few GREAT things happen without well-managed risk and the passion of greed to motivate the core human responses.

Unfortunately most men and women succumb to the greed impulse and find it burdensome to measure and account for the risks. Or, as you may have witnessed personally, some have been through a troubling scenario associated with

---

[2] *Wall Street (1987)*

unbridled greed and have retracted to becoming a more docile leader.

"Life can only be enjoyed by those who learn how to live."
rlt

The key to mitigating risk and obtaining your goals is to first prioritize what we'll call; the worst possible outcomes from this endeavor. If you are realistic about your list, you will find that there is no, off with your head decree. Nor is there a plight of world hunger or national publication that cares about the risk to your objective.

With that in mind, take a moment now to reflect on one of those times when you wish you had done something that may have made you uncomfortable, but would not have killed you. Now take that feeling and apply it to what you NEED to do to get your endorphins released, your mind responding positively and your sense of whom you are restored and invigorated. You must always focus on the **reward** and contain the **issues**.

Today's Challenges

The current economic slowdown is first and foremost at the top of the list of greatest risks to the current plan for most retailers. What pains were believed to have subsided into late 2009 and early 2010 have demonstrated extreme staying power in late 2011 through 2012 and the early part of 2013 in my estimation. This has had a tremendous negative impact across the entire retail industry as well as the emotions and behaviors of the general population. The pressure from reduced consumer spending and the option for more "value priced" merchandise has forced many retailers to cut costs from every corner of the organization. The balancing act for those organizations that will surface in 2013 and beyond as leaders is their ability to measure, mitigate and react to the factors of risk. No one will forecast with any semblance of accuracy, the direction of the consumer as they react to the daily, weekly and monthly stimulus. Therefore it is incumbent on the organization to maintain whom they are, why they're there and why will our customers shop with us tomorrow. When your decision tree takes you outside of one or more of those parameters, you have exceeded the boundaries of risk mitigation.

Many companies however have taken the extreme measure of cutting off their noses to spite their faces. As they begin to recognize the issues and potential resolutions, they're without captains to navigate the tumultuous retail waters ahead. In many of the recently released surveys, over a third of the retailers admitted to having the lowest amount or preparation for an economic slow down. Over half felt that they were genuinely concerned about potential damage to their reputation and brand. Another 50%+ assessed and found that they were at risk in the supply chain areas due to lack of knowledgeable personnel.

When you discuss risks, you have to acknowledge theft. In today's economy every company has to recognize that employee theft is a persistent and growing issue. The main catalyst for this growth is due to the mental anguish as employees battle job insecurity along with spousal layoffs and decreased spending power.

Keeping your associates engaged in the company's progress, efforts and what is more important, risk aversion strategies will go a long way to diminish their anxieties and bring forth the group effort to get through these times together. This of course is an ongoing process and should not be within a column of things to-do and check marked for posterity. Your plans for mitigating risk should be well documented, tested and understood by all. If the success of a project depends on the actions of a team, then the risks are magnified and will need to be managed accordingly. While there are no known packaged resolutions to all risks, there are a few things that you can do to assure the success of the project through even the toughest of times.

Communicate!   Communicate!   Communicate!

**That my friends, is how you understand
and handle risk!!**

Chapter 9

Clear Minds, Cloudy Judgment

When you've been affiliated with retail as long as I have, you get the chance to evaluate and recognize some of the more ridiculous beliefs that were originally presented as truths in the early days. Such is the case in one of the more common myths whereas the Buyer is autonomously declared the highest aristocratic position and their decisions are final. Although the buying position is a pivotal position in all retail establishments, the most sought after judgment and focus credentials for a buyer require a forward looking, aesthetic merchandise and market visionary. These qualifications are rarely accompanied by a strong mathematical, financial, systems and process aptitude. Thus require a team evaluation and informed relevant decision making at all times.

This domineering misconception has its roots in the deep recesses of the corporations of the past and simply where allowed to continue in today's businesses. No title depicts the abilities of the person occupying the position. Each person has their strengths and weakness and is valued for their ability to produce results and not their designated position.

Many senior executive members were once merchants or buyers and thus relate to the premise that the goods purchased are a reflection on the company that sells them. Today's corporations have to be more in tune with the reciprocal aspects of their offerings.   A much more sophisticated approach to merchandise procurement has been adopted and thus a more congenial approach is needed. The new normal behavior of a good merchandise buyer is to align their creative and emotional attraction of the merchandise with the intended consumer through pricing strategies as illustrated by their team members. The success of the buyer, and thus the corporation, depends on the synchronized relationships with the business tiered levels of associates in the organization.   Generally a planner, who provides financial and statistical wisdom necessary for analytical purchase decisions, a consortium of an allocation analyst, paired with a clerical associate who provides the foundation of business execution and progress levels. When this team is given the proper vision and held _accountable_ for the business under their umbrella, _responsible_ for their decisions, offered the process tools _capable_ of taking their individual actions and seamlessly create business team harmony, great business happens.

What happens in many business cases where failure is the outcome is that the eagerness to achieve individualized goals is met with an economically and physically constrained supply chain.   When pushed by an unreasonable amount of immaturity and ego by the buyer, the simple objective of obtaining the right merchandise for the intended consumer becomes an emotional compilation and disastrous results ensue. Without a defined process of SKU rationalization and category management, we are unable to see the classification _forest_ through the item _trees_. When individual items are purchased without an articulated and crafted roadmap, the merchandise doesn't make a statement or congeal as a classification representing the corporation's mantra. This action makes it difficult for the allocation, store and warehouse business units to make heads or tales of the intended consumer of these *random acts of purchase.*

However, as it is written in the retail bible; *a buyer is only as good as the last purchase they made.* This reinforces a buying mentality that more is better, hence Buying Right *and left.* Many merchants conveniently ignore the road signs that indicate impending danger and attempt to buy their way clear of foreseen obstacles. They accept slight cost increases and delayed delivery from their vendors in an effort to solidify relationships and minimize their own workloads of having to replace a commodity. These issues are evident in an organization where you find that purchase orders are consistently revised and your systemic tracking mechanisms are absent or derelict in alerting the right people. You would preferably relinquish this duty to someone who recognizes and understands the direct impacts on your labor force and is not concerned about a potentially strained vendor relationship when the original agreement has been, or is about to be breached.

Many organizations have brick and mortar stores or websites that are over assorted by as much as 25 – 30% if you believe some of the market research white papers. There is also some evidence that the more choices offered to the consumer in certain categories results in reduced sales. The consumer quickly becomes overwhelmed in their decision making process and postpones the purchase for a later date. The holding and handling costs associated with an expanded category are often the differentiator between positive and negative profit margins at the end of a cycle. The key for a successful merchandise inventory campaign and optimization pivots on the ability to intelligently rationalize your stock-keeping units, better known as SKU's against your profit and space capacity fluctuations.

In today's technologically advanced environment, there are plenty of systems to help you manage this process. But, none of them can conceptualize the intent of your organization's goals and objectives with the products to be offered. It is imperative that you receive and understand the key objectives for your area of purchasing. If doubt exists, write down your thoughts in a simple (3) three-point format and present them to your supervisor. Their feedback will help resolve any potential future issues of direction and controls.

Before you can get the area to where it needs to be, you must first assess where you are today and to some degree, how did you get here. A quick way to analyze your business is to take all the items that have sold for your area of responsibility for the past (9) months and rank them in order of performance. Take the top 15% and call them **Priority**, take the next 25% and call them *Necessity* and then take the next 45% and call them *Needed*. The remaining 15% are what I call **Next;** they have either been voted on negatively by the consumer or outlived their usefulness in your assortment.

Now a quick review of the average selling price for each of the buckets you just created will illustrate your optimal pricing strategy and assortment deviation. The larger the variance to your overall average, the greater elasticity you will have in your promotional offering. We will cover this exercise at a later time in more detail. Just know that the reward comes from quick, thought provoking analysis. Not mind numbing, reality obscured analysis paralysis that tends to overwhelm and confuse most.

Keeping your assortment tight and focused helps in many ways. You control your vendor community who often conspire to add layers of their products to your company's offerings. You also provide your distribution, allocation, planning and store associates with the ability to concentrate on the business drivers and not just getting their restocking job done. Now, I am not saying that you shouldn't have a variety of fresh product. The lifeblood, and the sustainable success of your company is dependent on fresh time and company relevant product offerings to attract new customers and to keep your core customers coming in. My advice is to create a somewhat static display mentality to your approach for an optimized fresh and enticing assortment.

Imagine that the items you just evaluated fit only on a static display unit, like a mannequin, or four-way or even a 4-foot shelf. You cannot show the latest and greatest new offerings unless you get rid of what is there now. You will need to liquidate a rolling (10% – 15%) of your assortment quarterly at a minimum. The best consultants and software vendors will illustrate this to you as a Product Lifecycle.

Your product lifecycles need to be an integral part of your merchandise assortment and flow process. Planning will play a key roll in preparing your data, you as a buyer or merchant are then responsible for turning that data into commodity driven concepts and products for your consumers. To become a truly successful buyer, your product choices, pricing, display and lifecycle have to be YOUR responsibility. You more than likely have been conditioned to find fault everywhere but within yourself. *The reason my area isn't as great as it should be is:* weather, the economy, the vendor, the planner, the allocation analyst, your boss, their boss...anyone and everyone but yourself.

You can make the difference! Many times we find comfort in pointing the accusatory finger away from ourselves into the most plausible arena nearby. Take control, as you have many times in the past, when you feel the urge to respond negatively about your associates and peers. If there is a problem that you, or someone else has identified, own the problem and resolve the issue. Positive enforcements determine the outcome of your decisions even when you have passed the baton to the next appropriate business driver in the organization.

The alternative is that you choose to keep doing what you've always done and you will keep getting the same results. Until you change, *the people and situations that drive you to drink will meet you in the bar.* You have to want something different from your area of responsibility to get the change you desire. You will be amazed how differently people respond to you when you illustrate the issue and solicit input and accept guidance and assistance.
Your purchases and product lifecycles will be so much more enriched when you become leader of your destiny and not a product of circumstances. Take time to do the right thing, and by take, I mean MAKE! Facing each day and each unpleasant situation head on will take you from where you are to where you want to be.

When delivering your synopsis watch for the body signals of your team as you discuss each situation. These yellow alerts should be cause for you to pause, regroup and amend your approach to the issue. Don't hesitate to solicit comments and questions from the crowd; you'll be glad you did. Be sincere and decisive in your discussions, each member of your buying team must realize that you are prepared to *take the blame and share the fame* in this endeavor. Your response to this change will be far more rewarding than you can imagine. You and they will be catapulted to a new level of creativity and understanding.

You can either orchestrate this new line of merchandise and environment in the light of your own knowledge and comfort zone, or allow things to be orchestrated for you. Use all the resources available to you; market, vendor and historical data. Customer trends, relational product offerings and directional indicators will supplement your decisions. But most of all, get to know your value and commit yourself to being the best at what you do by using others to ensure you buy right.

Short Term Goals & Long Term Objective

Which came first, the *goal* or the *objective*? For many years, retail pundits have vacillated on the proper use of these two terms. I am here to set the record straight conclusively. As decreed in the "New Oxford American Dictionary", the term; GOAL refers to - *the object of a person's ambition*. Whereas the term; OBJECTIVE clearly refers to - *a thing aimed at or sought; a goal.*

There you have it, either one is perfectly acceptable when illustrating the steps and course of action to take you from where you are, to where you wish to be. For instance, a long-term goal might be decreed to increase your market share in a particular category over your key competitors.

The Marketing division will support your efforts with more targeted advertising of your category. The planning area may give more focus on turn. There efforts may move towards a more heightened promotional and markdown strategy as opposed to typical historic measures of strictly reducing inbound inventory. To be successful, the key strategy is to collaborate and record your top 5 long-term goals for the business. In today's economy and climate, anything past 3 years is pushing your ability to carry out a truly meaningful objective. Remember that anytime you begin setting long-term goals your focus should be on the corporate vision. Either to sustain your current standings in the market place, or become more of a controlling entity. The vision has to be a clearly defined, obtainable and measurable congruently illustrating the road map from which each area of the company will **D.R.I.V.E.** That is, they must have individual and correlating business unit goals that are: (**D**irectional, **R**easonable, **I**nspiring, **V**isible and **E**ventual).

One of my favorite exercises has always been to announce the governing corporate objective to three or more symbiotic business units at the same time. Require them to go off and hypothesis their involvement and related expectations in achieving the objective. Reconvene the groups in (2 – 3) days and have them list their top 5 interpretations on parallel white boards.

What I often found was that each business unit walked away with a measurable increase of awareness of how and when the interaction of one unit impacts the other. Although you will find areas where they are very similar, the rankings are often distorted. You will also find that there are typically more areas where a serious conflict to achieving your goals is uncovered. Discuss these areas of discontent first to enforce the theory that all issues will be resolved with attention to area impacts and that everyone shares responsibility in the discovery of amicable solutions.

Once you are comfortable that the corporate objective has been harmoniously assessed and established, you are now ready to begin implementation of short-term goals and measurement points. Setting such goals will be challenging and much more difficult because now you are establishing timeframes and terms by which your management team will be held specifically accountable.

Where most companies fail is their lack of follow through on a timely basis. Questions like; when will the first phases of production increases begin? What is our basis for measuring the increase? How soon will we be able to resolve any deviations to our goals when discovered? Too many times the *experts* are left to their own demise of either achieving or failing their assigned tasks. That's fine if we are talking about their rolls within the organization...but we are often talking about an impact on the entire company. Hundreds and sometimes thousands of associates' livelihoods are reliant on the success of each and EVERY part of the plan.

You want to have the ability to review the short-term objectives to ensure that they are **S.M.A.R.T.:**

1. **S**pecific as to illustrate *exactly* what needs to be accomplished by whom, when and why.
2. **M**easurable and not just done or not done, but quantifiable by each participating unit's degree of completion and relationship to a specific goal.
3. **A**ttainable from the very beginning this has to be recognized by the majority of the team. If

dissension occurs in the ranks due to lofty unobtainable expectations, you've lost the war.

4. **R**eward each level of met expectations. This single motivating factor will return your efforts 4-fold. Be creative, have fun with the rewards but keep in mind that the ultimate goal is completion.

5. **T**imed in a sequence that allows each of the business units to complete their individual objectives creating a pyramid of success.

Think of the process of building a house. You have many different subcontractors who need orchestrating to finish the house in a timely and sustainable manner. You can't have the plumber in after the concrete foundation has been poured. It is too late for the electricians if your drywall team finishes their duties first.

Each business unit of your corporate team is a separate entity in need of direction and follow-through to complete the objective. This holds true within the individual business units where resources are occasionally needed from Information Services, Human Resources and the never-ending executive decision that's needed from time to time.

Although everyone can agree on an overall objective, how each one gets there is commonly different. When the long-term objective is announced to let's say, increase the inventory turn by (75) points this year and another (25) points consecutively each year for the next three years. Without our above S.M.A.R.T. process, conflicting goals are sure to appear.

For instance:

- Merchandise and buying business units view this as a need to reduce overall purchases.

- Store operations and marketing teamed up to discuss ways to alleviate aged and outdated product at the individual store level.

- The executive team felt that the best way to accomplish this goal was to shift the mix of business more towards the higher margin fashion and opportunistic in and out product, away from the basic commodity offerings.

Conflicting goals are common in businesses that choose to dictate their wishes without rationalization, follow a non-relevant leader in the industry like Walmart...*you just can't do what they do*, or refuse to humble themselves into recognizing that some of the individuals in charge don't always know what's best for the organization.

Many a wonderful organization has fallen victim to the new regime of executives who bring years of wisdom and knowledge of what they've DONE, not what is NEEDED. Rather than take the opportunity to listen and learn from the established associates, egos tend to usurp logic and conflicts are illustrated as the finger pointing begins and it's the other guy's problem and fervent mediocrity becomes a result.

The sooner you as a leader are capable of recognizing the area of disconnects within your organization, the better chance your team has for salvation. Sometimes you need to accept the fact that you don't know what you haven't experienced or envisioned and soliciting consultants can be a business life extension.

Keep your wits about you and know that if you're confused about your short-term goals and long-term objectives, many of your peers and associates are also confused. The better person isn't always the one who wins the battle, it's the one who in their mind have already looked two issues ahead of this battle and have successfully prepared their team to win the more important war.

Chapter 10

Time For Change: Why?

Socrates, the Greek philosopher, once replied to a question as to the need for change with; *Perfection is constant change.* Retail, which is always in pursuit of perfection, therefore must also succumb to the forces of constant change. For the past several decades the retail business cultures had become stagnant to the rapidly changing economic conditions. After evolving ever so slowly, there became acclimatization for rote processes that replaced the maverick ingenuity that once thrived. This mechanized methodology was homogenized and companies followed the academic buzzwords and acronyms, and even went so far as to duplicate processes as they proudly and purposefully marched to the beat of the *same* drum.

O.T.B. or open to buy, sometimes referred to as the checkbook for the merchant organization, was one of the most common rote adaptations in the early 80's for most companies. As I will discuss in detail in later chapters, the early renderings of the open to buy became a self-fulfilling process for mediocrity at best. The process included initial business performance assumptions that were based on a small trend or pattern to the same relevant time period last year. This myopic view was generally adapted six months prior to the current fiscal year end. The merchandise financial plan line of the open to buy is the foundation by which the budgeting activities for the New Year are launched.

Believe it or not, a hauntingly close faction to this practice continues in some form or fashion even in today's most intellectually savvy corporations. Even though it has been documented that 87% of the time, the basis of the original plan line for sales and inventory, is off by 28% or more just three months prior to year-end.

Using January as your fiscal new year in a routine planning session means an inventory plan would be completed around June of the current year. That year ending inventory number let's say is one million dollars to make it simple. That would get locked & loaded as your plan. By September of the same year the forecasted trend would have your year end inventory target coming in now on the high side at {$1,280,000} and on the low side at {$720,000}. The 28% margin of error has been accepted as *normal* in the retail community. To offset the critical financial issues surrounding a blind flight into the next fiscal time period, a *current plan* line was introduced to supplement the target process.

It is time to revamp this mind numbing; data gathering heresy exercise and replace it with a more robust structure reflective of current trends. By the mid to late 90's the focus gradually shifted to analytics and forecasting. With this transition came a new group of vendor applications, resident experts and processes that became so complicated that product, consumers and pricing became more of a by-product or afterthought and less of a focus.

Although most corporations were looking for the right answers by taking a deeper dive into their surface information, they grossly underestimated the relinquishing of general business logic. Analysis Paralysis was the prevailing answer towards even the most general and basic of questions. The statistics provided by using the power of technology became overwhelming to many new retailers and the true art of the business was abandoned.

This new economy has dictated a reengineered philosophical premise as it relates to projections, planning and budgeting. The long-term process of three to five years that was so much a focal point has now been converted to a three to six month assumption based forecast. The requirement now is to have a contingency plan for a minimum of three variables, which are mainly centered on inventory, sales and gross margin or profit dollars. Any deviation from the forecast requires a *plan B* for ensuring a healthy gross margin return on inventory investments, commonly referred to as G.M.R.O.I.

In the past there was a laser focus on the weekly issue at hand. If sales were down, the question was how quickly could you get the sales increased? If the Inventory was high, the question was how quickly could you get the inventory down? And if your gross margin was waning, you were either instructed to reduce discounts or increase retail mark ups. Today's more sophisticated practices are more equipped to recognize the tri-factor of each of these deviations to the plan and encompass a more holistic approach to resolving the variances. Knowing that the consumer demands value, loves a deal and has a buy now mentality has given opportunity to a new breed of retail gurus who understand the dynamics of the supply chain and the effects of a diverse and ever changing marketing campaign.

Relying on the way you use to handle issues and problems in no longer an option. A new way of evaluating the cause and effect so that the resolution doesn't shift the burden of reconciliation from one department to another is paramount. The best practice models are reliable as a guideline or basis for a solution as they too relied on normalized business standards. There isn't anything standard or normal about today's economy and thus requires a brain trust to ensure sustainable results.

Recently, several key companies like Macy's and The Limited became early adapters to the changing retail environment and met it head on with *times appropriate* differentiated business practices. What was considered relevant no longer had a mathematical equation; these leaders are focused on the micro managing of the business at the individual demographic and store level. Quickly reacting to the consumer demand patterns and creating actionable information where it was once lost in the layers of data and decision process at the home office.

Now here we are, in the midst of the most traumatic economical downturn our generation will ever witness, and many companies have not yet recognized the need to change leadership to thrive on the other side of this ordeal. When it comes to business, I am a perfectionist and wholly recognize that to arrive at a level of certainty and confidence, you have to travel the road of early rote disciplines. Much like a great athlete, musician, dancer or seasoned executive you have to learn, and commit internally the basics very early in your endeavor so that it becomes second nature in your thought process.

This can be taxing and tedious to say the least, but essential to your ability to take your *game* to the next level. Such is the case for retail at this juncture; it is time to take the game to the next level. No longer is the guiding principle that got you here applicable to take where you need to be. *Quick sustainable* is now an oxymoron, although a short time ago it was believed to be the mantra of many leaders in retail establishments.

It is imperative to recognize that during these tough, uncharted economical times customers will demand that you cheapen your offerings and lower your standards of quality to match their cost expectations. The leaders, who are able to rationally navigate their corporations through these short-term rapids without major changes to their creed, will be amongst the few long-term captains of the industry.

While many organizations will reach for a new system to help facilitate the necessary change, they soon find that the majority of systems only encapsulate and regurgitate their current policies for doing business. To change, you must employ the right people and have a focused agenda of what you wish to accomplish. Unless you are blessed with talented individuals in your company that have the passion, ability and knowledge to predict and prevent issues, you'll want to obtain outside expertise.

In search of retail utopia

When it's all said and done, utopia within the realm of retail is an exuberant state of mind obtained through a combination of surpassing financial objectives, sustaining or enhancing your corporate brand and broad consumer acceptance of new product introductions. Statistically, when your organization is able to sustain high single to low double digit comparison store growth over 8 consecutive quarters or more, with less than 10% aged inventory, 12 - 15% annual fresh product introductions and less than 15% personnel leadership turn-over during the illustrated period.... *welcome to utopia.*

Although the aforementioned are lofty goals for most retailers, one cannot deny the fundamental impact to your bottom line when these objectives are achieved congruently. Many organizational leaders fail to realize that it is the *trifecta* of accomplishments that must be achieved to experience retail utopia; sustained comp store growth, inventory optimization and personnel longevity that hold the key to success. They tend to set their goals on one or two of these objectives with total disregard to their symbiotic harmony and thus they unknowingly disrupt the balance need for a sustained growth pattern.

A more common issue is the establishment of different and deflective goals at one hierarchy of the company from another. Often I find that an area of a company, lets say allocation and replenishment, have a store inventory turn objective for their distributions that has no corresponding relationship to gross margin return on investment goals assigned to the merchant organization. This is typically because the allocation and replenishment areas deal in unit controls, not the value thereof, thus the focus is driven by pure consumer demand patterns on cheap non-margin generating commodities.

Over the last decade, while working with some extremely intelligent associates, software vendors and adorned university professors, I have developed a process called **Looking Glass™**. The procedure encompasses a basic set of control factors to ensure all objectives for the business quadrants of the organization meet at the epicenter or goal central. At the very core of this process are meaningful guidelines and measurement tools to help focus individual efforts and alleviate production inhibiters.

The premise is unadorned, the results are powerful, and the success rate is a testament to the simplicity of the rules of engagement. Based on the principle that *change is inevitable*, the acronym derived from the initial process reflects the need to be able to randomly assess your organization's opportunities and obstacles and turn on a D.I.M.E. As the saying goes; *in retail, you either change or you die.* I believe the person who first uttered those words was a part of the great Wal-Mart brigade of the '80's. Here are the keys to my change with a purpose theory:

1. Define the need; not just growth; but how much? How fast?
2. Identify the information requirements.
3. Measure historic accomplishments and know your limitations.
4. Engage social performance analysis looking for your *red herring.*

Now lets delve into each of these four part measures and get to know the cause and effect of decisions and why most of them cause more issues than alleviate problems.

Define the need: This process is literal in nature, but philosophical in reaching an amicable conclusion. By deploying controls against what are typically broadly defined problems, you can quickly assess whether a business unit is deflecting their own issues onto another, or we have a genuine issue in need of a resolution. For instance;

"the allocation team states that they _always_ receive too much initial receipt inventory and are forced to ship to stores without proper replenishment results and analysis."

Too many times this comment gets little to no attention and is regarded as whining. The key is the quantitative analysis approach that demands a more serious review.

"In the last (4) months, forty-five percent of all initial merchandise receipts were received with thirty-eight percent more units than needed to provide stores with initial setup quantity and five weeks of forecasted sales."

Now action can be taken and a resolution can quickly be instilled.

Identify the information requirement: To fully understand and thus produce a resolution to an issue, you must recognize the data source and ability to obtain *usable* data in your research. Too many non-productive hours are spent *chasing the tail* of the first dog in the pack and not determining the continuity of the data or information to your specified issue. When done properly, you will have established my *Triple know* policy on information.

1. *Know* where the proper data resides.
2. *Know* how to get to it and enable it.
3. *Know* when to use it to illustrate measurements.

Measure historic accomplishments: This one is vitally important and is juxtapose to the fourth entry in this process.   Using target data and process engineering standards, you will need to gauge the team's ability in the past to resolve issues. The premise of this will establish a barometer against the magnitude of the impending issue. It is one thing to gather and measure the data, it is an entirely different situation to analyze, confirm and use sophisticated tools and quantum mathematics to deploy proper solutions.

In general, if your team is measured on an accomplishment historic scale to be a **6** out of **10,** and your issue requires a level **8** to be resolved efficiently, you have a probability of success factor of **72.9%.**

Engage social performance analysis: This is where the rubber meets the road and performs with traction or skids on a wet, oily surface.   Many sustainable resolutions require a *passing of power* so to speak to another business unit in the organization. This can sometimes be a source of great embarrassment and angst for shallow department heads and their teams. In companies who have allowed the hierarchical silo business units to control their own destiny tend to fair the worst in this analysis.

Your goal early on in this process is to test the waters with the leadership in the organization by introducing some scenarios of change that would involve the relinquishing of duties to another more suitable area. Should you find resistance to your scenario during your inquiry, do not underestimate the impact this will have on your end results. Deal with it immediately as it will need to be addressed before continuing.   The only sustainable solution is ultimately one that the team chooses and adopts as their best resolution.

By recording the team's answers in the assigned tolerance scale, you will gauge the acceptance factor to be applied in the final evaluation to establish the time and action charts. Do not underestimate the dynamics between the acceptance factor and the ability to deploy a sustainable resolution. Many consultants have established a bad reputation due to the ineffective use of best practices and industry standards with organizations that have not yet achieved a harmony between where they wish to be and the effort needed to get there.

To drown an organization in statistics and numbers that lack direction and insight is a genuine disservice. It is just as arrogant to deploy level 4 strategies in level 2 companies that lack both the personnel and systems to obtain such a parallel.   That is why I devised the different phases of Looking Glass ™, which gives clarity of the steps needed, and the necessary policies and procedures to obtain utopia.

Contrary to popular belief; data proliferation is not the single most important factor to resolving issues and capitalizing on opportunities, it is only the basis for such discoveries.   Data must be converted to actionable information quickly and seamlessly to be effective. Point-of-sale data, commonly called (POS), inherently has been utilized at the (SKU) or Stock Keeping Unit level for evaluation and planning purposes. This process is void of the increasingly necessary detail components of the individual store, day and sell-thru data needed to recognize intricate selling patterns and profile attributes. It is this scientific evaluation of the data that can truly catapult a retailer from good to great and separate them from the pack.

The pain of developing good decision making practices and the time needed to condition the organization to follow said policies is temporary, the poor results of quick, data anemic emotional business decisions is forever.

Chapter 11

The Daily Grind
(Part: 2 of 3)

"Wait a minute, are you telling me that **none** of my *front* page circular Christmas merchandise items have left the warehouse yet?"

Just as Norman uttered this question to an unsuspecting allocation analyst, and an innocent emancipator of information, Mr. Treier came around the corner ripping the glasses from his now scowling face!

"What's this?"

He barks as he delivers a glare first into the allocator's eyes and then to Norman! Norman crosses his arms over his chest and lifts his chin ever so slightly towards the ceiling.

"Tell Mr. Treier what you just told me Michelle." Norman states in a concerned yet *{wait until you hear this}* voice.

As Michelle delivers her news directly to the CEO of the company, her voice trembles slightly as if somehow this could be her fault. Forty-five seconds into her story she concludes with,

"That's all that I know as of 8:30 this morning, sir."

Mr. Treier folds his glasses, puts them ever so gently into his breast pocket, smiles at Michelle and says;

"thank you Michelle, how are Lilly and Bryant doing in school?"

Wide eyed and without even thinking about the fact that here is a man with 10,000 associates in 46 states with financial pressures and countless decisions to be rendered daily, and he not only remembered that Michelle has kids, but their names too.

Michelle replies; "Great…just great, thank you for asking sir."

Her feelings of loyalty and purpose are abundant at this moment.   Unlike *the tool*, Mike Thompson, there are leaders in this company that make your hard work and effort worthwhile.

With a nod and a smile, Mr. Treier turns his shoulders and his attention towards Norman, raises one eyebrow and calmly states with his head tilted to one side;

"O.K. Norman, what are **WE** going to do with this little tidbit of information?"

Norman gives a half smirk to Michelle;   "Thank you Michelle, would you see if there are any new developments with our marketing request to Bob?"

Norman wasn't the least bit interested in the developments from marketing as he requested of Michelle, truth be told, he hadn't thought past the *pointing of the finger* why the holiday merchandise for next week's promotion was still in the warehouse. And he certainly hadn't thought through a plan of action.

However, being the consummate professional that he is, Norman replied;

"I will have the team pull together a list of all the promotional merchandise that *should* have been shipped by now for all departments and verify the items with Rickie."

Rickie Starnes is chief operating officer for the organization.   He knows more about logistics and transportation than most people know about their spouses. He's controlling, but enforces a work, life balance in his direct associates that is appreciated and rewarded with loyalty.

"Once Rickie and I have covered and verified our findings I will email you the results and an action plan if needed." Norman states.

"If needed? So you don't think that Michelle is telling the truth?" asks Mr. Treier

"No sir, it's not that.   I believe that whatever report Michelle referred to does *indeed* show that the merchandise is in the warehouse. I just want to ensure that the data on the report is correct." Mike replied.

Snapping his left arm from his side and bearing his left wrist to reveal a beautiful Movado watch, Mr. Treier says:

"It's 10:45 a.m. now Norman, how quickly can you get back to me with some answers?"

"I'll have a documented answer in your box by 1:00 p.m. at the latest." Mike said in a convincing tone as he gazed at the clock on the wall above Mr. Treier's head.

With a nod and a wink Mr. Treier proudly taps Norman on

the shoulder twice and mutters; "good man" as he turns towards the elevator and heads to his office.

Now The Fun Begins!

Norman returns to his office and takes a quick review of his appointment calendar to find that he has not one; but three back to back to back meetings starting at 11:00 a.m. this morning.

He quickly sends a *decline meeting response* from his Outlook to the meeting coordinators and the respondents. Simultaneously as he clicks on the last one, he reaches for his phone and places a call to Rickie.

"Hey Rickster, what's up?

"No you da man!" Norman says mockingly to the victim on the receiving end of the call.

"Here's the deal, Treier got word that we have front page promotional merchandise that hasn't shipped from the distribution center and he wants me to put together the facts."

Norman pauses for a second only to hear; "What the hell?"

Rickie blurts out as the background sound of paper shuffling and a chair screeching back from a desk replaces voices in the phone's earpiece.

Norman surmises that if the information is found to be true and it has anything to do with the D.C. personnel proudly leaving at 4:00 p.m. everyday, then he is talking with a *{dead man walking}*.

Rickie and Norman have never been best of friends. They

admire each other's abilities and the strengths that portray in their respective positions.   But, let there be an opportunity to tarnish either of their reputations and that opportunity will be taken.

"Hold on big guy." Norman says in a more calm and confiding voice.

"That's why I'm calling you. I want us to get some data together, have you and your team verify the findings and go from there."

Before Norman gains too much comfort in his assumption that it is not his issue, Rickie ignites Norman's adrenalin pump with;

"Well, did the allocation team get the distributions done in time?"

"You know if they didn't complete the distributions until Wednesday last week, we wouldn't see them here until today and you wouldn't see movement on your reports until tomorrow."

Rickie is sharp, and knows what to say when he is cornered.   Knowing this, Norman quickly defuses the allegation.

"That's what we need to find out here Rick. I will have an Excel list sent to you via email listing the item number, distribution slot license number, quantity shipped and the date released to the warehouse. Have your guys fill in the shipped from D.C. date and the quantity per daily wave."

Up to and until that point, Norman had only *assumed* that Michelle had completed her distributions in a timely manner. Now he has a potentially damaging issue on his lap because everyone knows that ultimately it is the

Buyer's responsibility to ensure that his or her merchandise is received, allocated, shipped and sold. Basically, until the customer buys the merchandise, *it's their baby*.

They are however given special dispensation in regards to the transportation, logistics and store maintenance of the displays. Outside of that, any issues will put them on the receiving end of the frantic calls, rants and raving why, how, when and where; *this could happen*?

"You guys still running five waves per week out there?" Norman asks.

"Yeah, we only change the schedule during holidays and physical inventories." Rickie replies in a sarcastic, *you know this,* voice.

"O.K., great! We'll have the sheet to you in the next 15 – 20 minutes." Norman blurts.

"Do you think you can get this back to me by say, 11:30 or a quarter till?" Norman requests.

"Hey…Hoe…what's the rush here kemosabe? Rickie asks in a half chuckling manner.

"Treier wants the report and any needed actions on his desk by 1:00 p.m. **today**!"   Norm states in a {that's why} dialect.

Now Rickie smells a RAT, he knows that Treier doesn't *give* deadlines, but he absolutely *holds* you to the ones you give him.

"No problem, you get us the list; we'll take care of the rest." With that comment Rickie closes the conversation with. "Later."   Before Norman can return the salutation,

Rickie hangs up.

Norman looks into the receiver as if Rickie can see him and bites down on his lower lip while squinting his left eye; **You son of a b-----!**

Now, It's on!

Do You Know This Guy?

Mike Thompson has what is commonly referred to as an *Eddie Haskell* complex.

Those of you scratching your heads not knowing who Eddie Haskell or what Leave it to Beaver is, you need to seek knowledge and wisdom from someone (35) or older.

You see, when it comes to dealing with his peers and associates versus upper management, Mike becomes two distinctly different people. He's caring and nurturing to the teams when in the presence of executives, but when he's not governed by the presence of someone in authority, you can hear his familiar voice and chants…

"You stupid *blank*"… "Get a brain; you *blanking* moron"

"Tell me your parents had at least one child that made it past the sixth grade!!"

Then, as abruptly as it began, you hear an opening remark from this same putrid of a man to the rhythmic shuffled steps heard faintly at first, and then growing louder in the hallway to the left, which flanks the parking deck:

"Good morning Mr. Johnston, nice sales yesterday huh?"
Mike raises two arms in a referee's field goal stance.

"I'd say we put that one right between the uprights!"

"Hope we have the wind behind our sails today to make
this a trend…"

"Yeah, from your lips to God's ears," says Mr. Johnston.

A rotund man in his late 50's, distinguished grey wings
outline both sides of his otherwise jet black head of hair.
He is the Chief Operations Officer and has been for the past
(22) years.   Everyone felt that he was headed for the
president's seat in less than (5) years after his appointment
to the COO position at the early age of (36).

Around the office, and out of the sight of the two engaged
in the conversation, you witness simultaneous fingers going
into mouths and animated gag reflex in harmony.   You
can't help but to agree with the symbolism.

Mr. Johnson tolerates Mike.   But make no mistake, when
push comes to shove, Mike will find that the last (15) years
of waiting and being overlooked for the presidency position
has psychological consequences.   Mr. Johnson won't be
capable of physically restraining his emotional eruption on
the unsuspecting soul that happens to trigger those
compressed emotions.   There is a pool going around 3:1
that it will be Mike at the other end of Mount Johnson's
eruption.

Mike isn't a _bad_ person, just misguided as to how he
appears to others. He is a product of his surroundings, the
expletive filled language and demeaning manner is how he
was introduced to the corporate world.   He was in the

Mesozoic age of store operations initially. Albeit brutal in the eyes of most human beings; that was just the way you were motivated to increase ones performance. He doesn't know any better and no one has yet challenged his attitude one on one. His defense mechanisms would be in full tilt should someone try to call him out in public.

What drives most people to criticize others is a lack of knowledge or ability to rationalize within. When you are confronted by one of these individuals, your best strategy is one that calmly and subordinately removes you from their presence. Each opportunity given is one that should be used to engage their more civil characteristics. *"I am not a barbarian, I can and do respond to intellectually superior stimulus."* Recite this to your evildoer(s), this gets them EVERYTIME!!

Now that the meetings are over you've once again witnessed the quintessential aftershock from a misguided attempt to reinvigorate your business doing the same things you've done in the past. You ran the same merchandise, with the same pictures and the same pricing using the same headline message and got the same response from your customers.

By definition, that is **insanity**; to repeat the exact *same* steps and expect a *different* outcome. Merchants and marketing executives tend to have a love affair with the processes that once gave them a sales and traffic high. They become addicted to the outcome and tend not to recognize the timing and/or the journey have changed.

"Good morning Nancy, is Bill in his office?" Norm asks in his professionally masked calm voice.

"He sure is, he'll be just another minute; the president is with him. Do you wish to hold?" she asks.

"Yes thank you." Norm replies with a smile and nod that she can't see.

Bill is the senior vice president of Marketing and E-commerce. His role has been elevated in the company, not because of his performance, but because his group is the creative avenue for attracting new customers. People are shopping less and saving more, not a great combination for a company needing to shore up their bottom line. The emphasis has temporarily shifted from product and pricing, to exposure and branding. Don't think that there isn't a symbiotic relationship here.

Online shopping and promotional events are the only two avenues that the customer is responding to favorably. *Show them value, create a sense of urgency and keep fresh new merchandise flowing*, declared the ($450) an hour consultant after speaking to the associates and disrupting the daily activities of the area for (6) weeks. Called in by the board, they took our top 10 ideas and rolled them into a 3-phrase mantra. *Nice work if you can get it.*

Bill has just been grilled by the president for what is *NOW* being deemed a haphazard attempt to portray the company's value proposition. Your company has (10) of the last (12) MVP Monday morning quarterbacks in the entire retail league. They have superhero hindsight vision coupled with an uncanny ability to instate an *I told you so*, when they actually didn't have a clue.

Although nothing is sent to press until EVERYONE in senior management signs off, selective amnesia has plagued the executive staff. There is a mad dash to the side of the stadium housing the winning team when there's only seconds left in the game. Funny how the views change after the customer has voted.

After holding the telephone line for what felt like 20 minutes, Norm reaches down and quickly pickup and drop the receiver to the base, severing the call which was on speaker. Norman's mind races between visions of what is transpiring between Bill and the president. No sooner does the receiver hit the base than Norman's personal ringer voice-over is activated; "You have a call!", then two seconds later, "You have a call!"; *everyone hates that ringer by the way.*

"Hey, Nancy said you called?" Bill exclaims in a shallow airy voice.

"Yeah, I was wondering if you have a copy of last year's holiday promotional fliers?"

Norm asks as if he weren't dying to hear the *play by play* of what just transpired.

"I have them, but you don't want to use them!" Bill replied in a sharp and *matter of fact* tone.

"The president just chewed me a new one for allowing, and I'm paraphrasing here, but he said:

" ***That *&$#@ merchant organization!*** Once again proved that they haven't a clue to what the hell our customer wants or needs!"

The phone goes silent, then without thinking; a smirk of a response escapes Norm's lips,

"Well if we **had** a clue, it was changed by their constant rebuttal chant of:

"What was your biggest success last year?"

And, who can forget the timeless classic statement of:

"This isn't rocket science people, keep it simple and manage your inventories!"

With that being said, all aspirations of trying new and different approaches to creating a destination shopping experience for your core and new customers dissipates in the wind.

"O.K. then", Norman says in a defeated voice and hunched shoulders.

"I guess I'll wait for the *new* and *improved* directions on how we need to pursue this fall's holiday promotions, Thanks Bill!"

And with that, Norman begins to tell his colleagues, who too are engaged in the procurement process of obtaining inventory contracts from their overseas factories and vendors.

With a minimum of a (6-8) month lead time, unless the commitments are established in the next (2) weeks, MORE hell will be paid for not having the product here on time!

You see, this is a vicious cycle of events and decisions that are played out in every retailer known to mankind. The curse of last year's performances is used as a backdrop for today's sales. There is no law of retail that predicates this as a rule, however it continues to persevere time and time again, with similar results.

Instead of using the results of last year in a copycat fashion, you will prolong your stay and ensure the proper trajectory of your company when you can analyze your current business trends and quickly evaluate your options for improvement. The first process is to analyze the impact of consumer centric demand patterns on a market basket of data, and then break it down to your area of responsibility.

"O.K. people!" barks Mr. Trent. "Here's the game plan!" making eye contact with each of his disciples.

" I want each department to list all items that had at least (100) units of sales in the last 6 weeks with (7) key columns of data representing each item. Along with basic item description, retail pricing, cost and vendor, I want the last (3) columns to show units sold, dollars sold and gross margin dollars.   Kim?" he yells, looking to and fro; he again yells, "Where's Kim Styler?"

A young lady with brown hair, studious brown-rimmed glasses and attire befitting a vice president raises her hand: "Here sir." Kim or *Mr. Trent's protégé* – as they call her around the office- is a **go to** kind of a person. Exceptionally smart, and exceptionally helpful, two attributes rarely found in a *cutthroat* retail office environment like the one created in the common merchandise area.

"Kim, you know what I'm looking for, put together an Excel template spreadsheet on the LAN and give everyone in this room access."   Mr. Trent states in more of a harmonious tone towards a colleague than a subordinate.

"People, I want this data pulled together in the next hour and a half." No one flinches.

"Rank the dollar column first, then the units and gross margin dollars. Although your list is based on selling at least (100) units in the last (6) weeks, I want (12) weeks of selling data."

He waits to see if anyone illustrates body language of being confused. His piercing eyes, deep voice and staunch presence demands attention.

"Then I want you to compare these items to the same ranking of items sold last year for the upcoming (3) months last year! Got it?"

Those who spent at least 6 months with Mr. Trent, you knew immediately where he was going with this exercise and began pulling your data. The process is one he deems; *quadrant analysis.* You take your findings, place them side-by-side and create analytical baskets by comparing the top (35%), the middle (50%) and the bottom (15%) from each list that compose and plot each quadrant.

This produces an indisputable grouping of consumer centric data tables that can be analyzed and filtered to reveal the strengths, weaknesses, opportunities and threats by department known as S.W.O.T. analytics. This silo information can and will be congealed into a corporate view for marketing and vendor evaluations.

...and they say he's just a man.

Chapter 12

Follow The Leader, Not The Position

One of the more common misjudgments known to retail is that the *position* itself dictates the level of *respect* and *admiration* to be bestowed and not the person who occupies the position. You will recognize the resemblance of traditional retail to a military group or dictatorship, which is where I believe this mentality originated. Unfortunately this mindset causes the great thinkers and mavericks amongst our associates to quietly relinquish their potentially better and more efficient ideas to the dictatorial supervisors and managers. A true leader is followed blindly without hesitation by his or her peers and associates. Now that doesn't mean that there aren't questions. However, intellect, respect and integrity ensure that the questions and/or concerns that are proposed by the team are geared towards *how* and not *why*!

While many of the leaders today find themselves attempting to think outside the box, sometimes the very nature of their issues are simple and don't require radical thinking. Occasionally you should try turning the knob before you prepare to knock the door down. Far too often leaders are convinced that their role in the organization is to come up with a new invention called the rounder wheel.

There is often no cause for reinvention or to be *innovative* when resolving a mundane basic issue.

What retail needs right now is much more influences from their resident experts, those who are the critical thinkers and possess the ability to creatively resolve complex issues quickly and effectively. These skills are more in demand today then ever before in recent history. The closest revolutionary industrial comparison to our current times is the likeness to the onset of the computer age. Most people could not envision the power of this new technology, but soon after they witnessed it they were pushing the engineers for more, faster and lighter versions of this thing called a computer.

With the uncertainty in the economy, the short-term decisions are more complex as they have long lasting repercussions that did not exist five to ten years ago. In today's retail environment it is not uncommon for your competition to literally use your promotion to point out how their product, pricing and/or service is better than yours. There use to be an unspoken gentleman's agreement in regards to such blatant displays of disrespect.

Unless your house is in COMPLETE order, do not antagonize the neighbors by pointing out their dust bunnies.

In short, *"he who is without retail sin may cast the first stone..."*

Organizations operate at a much different standard today, and along with that, have been lacking in the development of leaders who are prepared to resolve the complex, uncertain and volatile issues of today. The key reason for this is that the goal has never been set to create organizational savvy executives while driving the day-to-day businesses. The process has been for generations of retail executives to be told what to do and *what* to think as apposed to *how* to think and reward maverick endeavors.

As a means to better prepare our leadership in retail, I believe that it is time that our meeting escapades include a form of realistic challenges that the leaders and their teams will inevitably face. This practice is used abroad to sharpen the mental capacity and process integration contingency plans long before the need arises. Such preparation can provide a myriad of benefits while mitigating the redundancies of reliving last week's business dissertations and the pontification of what could have happened, only if. While the business of retail has changed, the process by which decisions are made, and plans are executed has predominately remained the same. 80% of the resources are dedicated in tandem with executing to a historical business plan, or developing short-term reactions based on recent results. My contention is that we would elevate our associate's acumen and realize a more robust and less volatile revenue progression if we instituted a more balanced ***60/40*** rule. Without this fundamental change, the business as usual premise will continue to permeate throughout the mediocre corporations.

The 60/40 rule simply dictates that for 60% of the time a leader allows his associates to devote their experience and expertise on executing the current plans and actions needed to operate the business. 40% of the time will be segregated into pragmatic exercises designed to improve the relationships and cognitive understanding of competent decision-making. It is during this time that the company will realize that the power of the decision lies in the process of empowering the teams to work towards an agreed upon outcome with little to no leadership intervention.

Retail has for years defined the role of leadership as *a commander that relinquishes the power of the decision to no one.* So when you look around at our leadership of today, for the most part, you identify the personality traits and behaviors in retail as self-induced. To be a better leader and create a better retail for tomorrow, the focus must be on accomplishing a balance between achieving the mission that has been assigned while vastly improving the organization's personnel and processes.

For as many years as there has been retail, there has been an unspoken rule that issues are resolved through the confides of a system or tribal knowledge in order for the endeavor to be successful. This has greatly amplified the amount of time and resources needed to correct inefficiencies and resolving impending issue. By placing such boundaries on your personnel you are all but guaranteeing that the way thing are, is the way they will be.

Now, many of you will regard this as a springboard to launch a new 60/40 best practice in your corporations. My cautionary statement to you is; *know your personnel, expected outcome and be prepared to identify and make changes.* Too many re-engineering projects fall short because of two main factors.

> **One;** leadership is required to fully understand and prepare their associates for the impending changes while establishing the rules of engagement during the process. This includes training the associates on time management. Giving them insight as to the niceties versus necessities in their current routines

as there will not be any additional hours assigned for the training exercises.

Two; Full circle communication and feedback. This means that questions cannot only be encouraged they must be required. Even if you allow the participants to remain nameless, they must submit questions that are reviewed at each subsequent meeting. This not only will foster a participatory learning environment, but also will act as a foundation for meaningful challenges and debates as the process begins to take traction.

As a leader, and what is more important a producer of leaders, your roll is not to manage people but manage the atmosphere to facilitate growth. Once you've committed to creating an environment for learning and unrestricted creative thought processes, increased business efficiencies and accelerated productivity will be byproducts. As the teams evolve and great leadership emerges, the organizational loyalty factor will also been increased. The pay for performance model can be replaced with a model of increased accountability, rewards with delegation of responsibility and promotions for the most active participants, which will result in the justifiable monetary increase.

To successfully lead a team of people, the leader has to address each situation with a focus on the group as a whole. The resident experts will reveal themselves and create a dynamic platform from which you can build. Creating answers to questions not yet asked is the epitome of arrival for any leadership campaign, as the team congeals this will become a standard as they ponder the issues of tomorrow while solving the problems of today. The successful leadership *for* tomorrow will recognize their roles in the industry as more of a coach and developer of minds, and will have converted their need and desire for hierarchical power into the power of developing others.

Lead your business endeavors with technology, don't be lead by the constraints or inabilities of your systems.

To optimize a company's strategic and financial goals, they MUST incorporate the use of advanced technology. If you thought that I was deemphasizing the use of technology, you would be sadly mistaken. The challenges facing the profitability and the very likelihood of a retailer's existence today, depends greatly on their understanding and ability to integrate the right technology. Regardless of how well thought-out the business strategies, the success thereof is counterbalanced on teamwork, instructions and technology. Business processes must work in harmony across multiple business units with little to no thought of doing so from the personnel. To do this, retailers must be operating time appropriate technology. My focus is on the proper convergence of technology based on YOUR Company's business, YOUR current and forecasted customer base and YOUR current associate acumen. You will also come to recognize my refutation of the very common corporate practice of implementing the latest and greatest technologies for the sake of saying you have them.

Most leaders underestimate the challenges associated with implementing new systems and business practices without examining the current organization. There have been many examples of (ERP) Enterprise Resource Planning overload. The vendors for these systems are extremely good at what they do and are able to sell the concepts to the executive teams by virtue of the system's capabilities. These systems _**DO**_ have the capability to create a common shared information warehouse from which all decisions can be unified. Each area's business decisions can be tested and agreed upon without constant time draining meetings and interventions from those who hypothesize the outcomes under a pessimistic umbrella. Pure, clean mathematical equations based on current trends, future goals and resources. SWEET!

Now for a dose of reality! That software was never designed to optimize the way YOU do business. The lure of better margins with fewer markdowns, less open orders, more sales at regular price and a decree of optimization of everything from the vendor's floor to your sales floor is just too titillating to pass up. Here's the deal! Engineers in a vacuum design the majority of your ERP packages using some industry experts and a few case study participants that embark upon a self-fulfilling journey. They congeal on some best practices used by successful retailers and convert those findings using state of the art software and slick user interface modules.

Don't get me wrong; I have nothing but love for the vast majority of software vendors. There are those however that first practice to deceive, and then structure a maintenance model that makes it impossible for you to leave.

The processes embedded in these software packages are by design constructed to cover thousands of retail best practices. By their very nature and business goal is to sell, and legitimately help, as many corporations as they possibly can with their product. There in lays the situation for many a best practices. Your alert to these potential scams will be when you hear that there are; *very little system configurations necessary*. This is a pretty good sign that your getting what I affectionately call *TOAST*, {*T*echnically *O*perating *A*s *S*imple *T*emplates}.

These templates on steroids are often structured to romanticize the efforts of streamlining processes and removing human intervention from the business of reacting to the numbers. That's all well and good, but you don't need a team and six months to get you there. The plausibility for a canned software package, off the shelf, that will mitigate your pain points while infusing your opportunities with little to no configuration is absurd.

First and foremost, the issues plaguing your business have to be recognized and illustrated in a hierarchical format and then agreed upon. The next step is to form a consensus on the expected outcome upon their correction. Particular attention must be made of the causal factor of each issue, being careful to illustrate that the problems are *intrinsic* to a condition that exists and not *contingent* upon such. This will keep you out of the deployment of cures for the symptoms, and allow for focus on addressing the issue.

It is at this juncture you will begin the prioritization of the issues and the who, how and when timeline of completion. A common malpractice is to attack the perceived biggest issues first. When mapped out properly using the technique of illustrating cause and effect, this becomes a rudimentary exercise in most cases. You will find that your leadership will be paramount while establishing a project template. Some will disagree with the premise, others with the resolutions. You must portray confidence and a willingness to listen while not hesitating with the delivery of your final judgments.

However, you cannot take the role of dictator. The quickest way to lose the battle for reinvigoration of the team and their processes is to attempt a *force-feed* approach. The project will tend to suffer from regressive tendencies and the associates will shoot holes in the project to go back to their old ways. I know, it is a juggling act; one that has serious ramifications if ANY of the balls hit the ground. A strategic decision that includes the introduction of technology is built on the premise of change. Those who are affected the most will be your biggest adversaries. Get them on board early and deep. Make sure they are in on the early discussions; even before the senior management executive decisions are evaluated.

Make sure that the technology that is chosen is based on its ability to enable your processes, mostly derived from associate input, to work efficiently. Not where the technology dictates a new way of operating a business, unless it is chaos you strive for. Drive home the sense of urgency to accomplish the tasks at hand. The opportunities to improve the current processes while reducing the manual labor aspects and accelerating positive results are components of a successful launch. You must not underestimate the power of tribal knowledge and the pursuit to do things the way they've always been done. Emphasis the expected results, and what is more important, when change can be expected.

Tell Them; Show Them; Then Tell Them Again.

A picture is worth a thousand words and a properly done timeline can show and say it all. A simple yet informative timeline can quickly and efficiently keep everyone apprised of the current game plan and what can be expected next. The main key for success, explain how issues that may impede the timeline will be resolved.

One of the greatest legacies with technology is that the very nature why we implement systems becomes the nature of our predicaments. We utilize technology to replace manual or redundant processes that require little to no expertise as well as those areas needing extremely sophisticated thought processes and intellect. Once the systems are in place, based on what we knew at the time, things change and we're left with a resounding shoulder shrug as to what next.

That is why my encouragement to you is to know your team's capacity for understanding and deployment of systems and process. Make sure that the sophistication of such doesn't put your company in a position of vulnerability, especially when it isn't necessary. For instance, a new allocation system should NOT bring your company to a stand still when a glitch occurs. You must always have a plan -B to deploy within a couple of hours. This rule of engagement should become your mantra with any deployment of technology from warehouse to finance. No one should sleep well at night knowing that newly introduced technology will be their ONLY means of getting their jobs done.

You must recognize that technology has its lingo and acronyms that can at times be confusing and frustrating for some to get their arms around. Too many half-leaders open and/or end their discussions with; if there is something you don't understand, please ask questions. Most people will hesitate to be the first to ask questions for fear of appearing lame or foolish. That's why I recommend, and make it a habit to speak in terms that is clearly understood by my audience. I do not dive into the technical aspects when addressing the teams as a group, and I do not speak about the individual item impact and relativity of gross margins when addressing the Systems personnel.

Technology in business, over the years, has become more than a tool to acquire answers and reduce the complexity of data manipulation. For many companies it has become the *end-all-be-all* of performance standards and the guiding principle behind decision-making. Although powerful, the information is often left in the wrong hands for interpretation and can often lead to disastrous results. This is most commonly apparent in the use of new technology that is implemented before the executives have clearly and concisely defined the current and future needs of the organization.

To operate successfully in this new economy, and what is more important the challenges that yet await your teams, you must first know and understand your business. Not just the ABC's of buying and selling, but the practices and principles of each of the business units needed to take your business to the next level.

Technology can't do that for you.

Chapter 13

Product Lifecycle Improvement

Everyone understands seasonal product lifecycles; they are dictated by the days on a calendar. But few rationalize the ebb and flow that should dictate the lifecycle of everyday products and new product introductions. What was once regarded as a standard operating practice, product lifecycle management (PLM) was dependent on a sales profile and a return on investment expectation assigned by a buyer/planner team. Those times are gone forever! The product evolutionary process is changing rapidly for retailers. That, which was once considered basic everyday products in the South, are considered seasonal product in the North. I'll take that one further, items once considered to be ethnic are now urban and have distinct selling patterns in rural area based on a given circumstance. As in the words of the great lyricist Robert Zimmerman, *aka Bob Dylan*; "The Times They Are A Changing!"

To maintain a sustainable competitive market advantage the processes by which your company identifies, organizes and controls a specific product line within a specific geographic and demographic area must change also. Product innovation is paramount to a successful consumer centric demand optimization campaign. Unique processes will be required to regulate the cost of introduction, and the rewards of consumption and customer support. Although private label programs have been the driver of bottom line improvements in the past, they will soon become the bane of your production and supply chain issues.

The foundation for improved PLM requires that a set of business rules, unique to your company and the commodity you're offering, be established. These rules are apt to change, and often times will, therefore a manual process will not suffice. Think of these rules as a set of indices that are established to govern a particular response from your management team. For instance, when a product's profile intersects a particular index, it will trigger an order, or markdown, or replenishment amount. The rules are based on your organization's turn, profit and supply chain capacity components.

To build and manage this process, a simple data warehouse with a mission-critical business intelligence platform will be required. These systems are abundant and reasonably priced from an array of vendors. Where most companies' fail in this process is in the separation of what the software is capable of doing, and how that interprets to their back of house systems and resources. The technology vendor community selling the system is genuinely interested in your success. However, like a fancy new smartphone, in order to get the most out of it you have to own or signup for the right data plan.

An initial place to form a firm foundation to achieving your goals is to take your current data and assign volume groups and attribute indicators by individual products and stores. By appropriating business indices you will be able to segregate the actionable issues from those that are just temporary and self-correcting. You will find some systems that require you to segregate your items in stores into nice neat buckets. This hard-coding will only leave your team wondering what went wrong at the end of the year when your inventories aren't optimized, your yard is full of trailers and your stores are jam packed with slow selling, low margin merchandise.

In managing your product lifecycle you will need direction on the *true cost* of goods sold. Not just the number of units sold of a given commodity multiplied by the purchase order cost, but the fully burdened cost including logistics and transportation, store operation, marketing and liquidation. If you don't have this operation in your organization today...get there! This process is critical to creating an even playing field by which your evaluations will determine the most logical and economical next steps.

Most retailers today have found ways to trim top-level costs out of their supply chain processes of getting goods to market. But unless you're the size of a mega-retailer, you won't continually enjoy the fruits of your labor in the months and years to come. Your vendor community is in a similar business to yours, they need profits to sustain payrolls, thus a cost increase will soon follow the savings you recently amassed. Knowing this provides opportunity to continuously improve sourcing and deal buying opportunities, which can reduce lead times and thus increase turn and allow for quick responses to changing consumer buying habits.

As the retail recovery takes shape and demand exposes itself to the new normal, a new era of operations will govern the process for profits. Because of the importance that private label merchandise will have on your company's bottom line and customer retention factors, contract negotiations will be paramount. Vendor relationships have been a mainstay in retail for years. The level of personal acquaintances rather than the vendor score card or quality of merchandise delivered generally defined a good relationship. Tomorrow's leading retailers will have adopted a much more statistical evaluation and introduced forward-looking collaborative platforms to streamline the issues and manage the exceptions. A vendor will occupy a preferred list ranking which will indicate the retailer's allotment of capital based on historical returns on inventory investments.

This process will not prohibit the humanistic side of the business and the personal relationships. It will however govern the amount of exposure any one vendor can have. Everyone will know the rules and the basis by which they can achieve a higher vendor ranking. This process is known as Collaborative Vendor Assessment or CVA as the initialism. The synergistic processes that will simultaneously drive new and more robust innovations are why you will not want to dismiss this change in your behavior.

The additional process improvements required will be in the reduction of stock-outs and overstocks. This age old inventory control battle has been fought on the most humble grounds of the smallest of enterprises to the behemoths that produce more than a billion dollars of revenue…DAILY! Consumers want what they like, and they like what they can't get. The answer to this puzzle is within your organizations mission statement. If you don't have one…well, there may be your answer. A great mission statement will encompass a little of whom you were, and relinquish any confusion of who the company wants to be. More importantly, it will direct all focus on the concept, pricing and availability of products in your portfolio.

Most executives know that 20% of the consumers that purchase their merchandise supply you with 80% of your sales. This has been, and will most likely always be true. So merchandise freshness takes on a whole new functionality within your product differentiation conversations. Although the key is to be less like your competition, it is more important to own the key items and create newness and freshness through size and improved formula offerings of that, which is proven. This will enable your product lifecycles to reveal a more centralized and strategic prowess by keeping the category from being overwhelmed with too many styles.

Breaking It Down!

In order for a company to improve the product lifecycle, they first have to illustrate and understand where they are today. I generally start by having the company supply me with an item file, or raw item data illustrating the SKU, stock keeping units, the Style numbers, which are often used as a sub-sub-category, and all of their classification information. Typically, I would ask for the last five years of history but considering the new economy and my applicable index basis to current trends, the last three years is plenty. With this data I can surmise the basis for some quantifiable sku rationalization, assortment planning and price optimization models. In the secondary phase of this process I apply the models to a superset of store volume and space charts that create an _aha_ moment for the teams.

Here is where I will be giving you a leg up on your competition, so to speak. To maximize your team's efforts and nourish their passion to create, you must create boxes for them to place their merchandise ideas into. I know that sounds counterintuitive to the mantra of thinking outside of the box, however too many inventory control efforts have failed because of this unbridled theory. I will explain in detail what this all means in later chapters, for now allow it to suffice that in the new process a box represents a part of your company's mission statement. Whether your company is in the value merchandise proposition or on the high-end luxury retail side, you must follow the same guiding principles of assortment rationalization. You must answer the questions of WHO is your customer, WHY should they shop, or continue to shop with you and HOW efficiently can you entice that consumer to share their wallet heavily with you in your product offering. These and many other questions can be easily summarized and then, and only then you will be ready to optimize your product lifecycle.

The textbook product lifecycle diagram will typically have a series of (5) five dimensions. Each future dimension developing from the one it precedes based on an agreed upon succession of triggers or conditions that are achieved. When illustrated properly, the simple process has a natural progression from development of the idea into a sellable product, and follows a cadence through the cycle of declined sales and final disposition. Lets take each level and break it down.

> **Development** – This stage of the cycle is the most critical of them all. You would be wise to have a minimum of (10%) of your item count in a development stage. If you are responsible for

(2,500) active items, then you should have a minimum of (250) items in the development stage.

Here is where the product has weathered all the assignment box tests including value to OUR consumer, costs and retail, vendor, country of origin and finally packs size and dimensions. Only after achieving an acceptable approval rating will the item be ALLOWED into the assortment. I use the term *allowed* in this process because too many times the decision to introduce new products are often based on emotion or feelings. Although *freshness* is essential to a retailer's livelihood, the introduction of the wrong product at the wrong price has more detrimental affects than just taking up space and inventory.

Introduction – How will this new product be introduced into your supply chain? Will you use a seasonality profile? Is the product going to be advertised? Is it purchased for only a preferred group based on geographic or demographic standards? These are the types of questions that must be answered and then shared with the allocation team prior to the formal purchase. Although the importance of the decision making process may be apparent to the purchaser, I cannot stress enough the importance of relaying this information downstream so that the effectiveness of the most PROFITABLE liquidation is not compromised.

Growth – Too often is the case that a new product is developed and introduced to the assortment and then relinquished to the forces of general retail. A new product must have a plan, a goal by which actions are triggered as the product lifecycle is completed. The growth face is a very important part of the lifecycle. Here the quick response to early indications can be the deciding factor between profitable longevity and premature losses. A guiding factor is the speed at which your product reaches and sustains a respectable unit movement based on the percentage of inventory sell-off. If your forecast assumed a 5% sell through of inventory at (500) units a week after the fourth week of existence, and you reach said goal on week number (2) two, your calculated growth factor will designate your next moves. You may need to increase future orders, move them closer in or cancel an assumed promotion to save margin. You, nor your team, will know what to do if you haven't illustrated your expectations for sales and inventory on a timeline commonly called a ladder plan.

Maturity – Once you have established your baseline from introduction to growth, you will then calculate what I call your maturity target. You can generally forecast your maturity target with a high degree of accuracy when you utilize my historical dynamic linear regression model. The goal is to begin your reduction of orders in conjunction with this target. You will enhance your gross margin return on investment by (25 – 30) basis points by following the controlled rules of engagement. The maturity of your product does not mean that there is an absolute end date to be assigned. It can simply indicate that you have reached critical mass and if profitable, you can maintain a respectable shelf presence as you continue to feed inventory into the sales.

However, the main focus will be on the level by which your product has matured. If substantially below your targeted return expectations, you will proceed to the last phase of your lifecycle. If the product is at or above your expectations, you will need to establish the proper funding and control the costs through negotiations with the vendor. A long prosperous product relationship is in the best interests of all parties involved; make it worth everyone's efforts.

Decline – This brings us to the final stage of the product lifecycle. Until now your goal was to ensure that the merchandise under your jurisdiction was profitable and raised as much revenue for your organization as possible. You are to handle the decline in the exact same manner. When you properly plan for the declining relevance of a product within an assortment, you will not only mitigate the markdowns associated with liquidating the final inventory, you will simultaneously be able to introduce the next new product from your development stable. Based on the production and profitability of the product, your liquidation process will enable a swift and clean process. The higher return you received prior to decline, the higher your first markdown and speed of subsequent marks will be allowed. Remember…your first mark should always be your best!

To achieve a fluid product lifecycle with minimal effort, you will want to read my next book; it will detail the aggregate steps to establishing all points of contention and the proper responses to these indicators. To improve the product lifecycle, you must understand two simple rules of engagement; 1) plan for failure early after the release of a new product, 2) act swiftly without emotions when the rules dictate a response.

Chapter 14

Inventory

Get More From What You Have

Inventory, when it is balanced and spot on with the consumer's wants and needs, it is sometimes regarded as the most valuable commodity a company can **possess**. Now you may have heard others in the industry call inventory the *second* most valuable asset behind your personnel. I prefer not to place our associates and inventory in the same evaluation bucket. People are far more valuable than the inventory assets we **possess** as retailers; and are certainly harder and more costly to replace.

Your inventory, for argument sake, in reality only really has two levels of operation. Sold, and in preparation to be sold. Anything else falls into a category I like to call *suspense*. The great retail leaders are not comfortable with the fact that they know, understand and teach their suspense factors. They are also an active and integral part of controlling the ebbs and flows based on a series of key performance indicators.

Having the right inventory available for your customers is a combination of art and science with science leading the way. People have always been in search of a reason to buy or not to buy. One of the biggest decision makers in favor of buying is the value proposition. The right price of your merchandise is rarely the first price, as the leaders of E.D.L.P. or Every Day Low Pricing found. Soon after these campaigns began, the customer found it more emotionally gratifying to shop the store that offered 40% savings occasionally over the one that offered 35% savings day in and day out.

The most overlooked process in controlling inventory is the cash to cash cycle. Which is a measurement of how quickly you convert the purchases of inventory into sales. Your supply chain practices play an important role in this efficiency measurement. Another component, albeit not as controllable, are the vendor terms for payment. The catalyst to influence the vendor terms for your purchase orders is the financial liquidity of the organization. However, for most vendors it is a standard operating practice to use similar terms for certain tiers of customers, judged mainly by the frequency and amount of orders.

Having visibility to your end-to-end supply chain practices will afford you the target for improvements. It is the old saying that you can't fix that which you cannot see. Retailers who have visibility of their supply chain, have better control of their inventory and cash to cash cycle times.

If your organization has poor visibility of your supply chain practices then you will have little control of your inventory assets. When confronted with this realization, many organizations fall victim to a series of costly investments into sophisticated software and consulting engagements. Before any external application can be introduced you must first condition your associates. The key to a successful turn-around campaign is to educate your personnel to recognize and understand the value of *behavioral change*. Until the organization recognizes the inhibitors to efficient and sustained inventory management, no system will guide the company to resolving the roadblocks to the flow of product to your consumers efficiently.

From years of trying different methodology and watching the inherent disciplines across a multitude of retailers and business professionals, I have adopted a successful process for resolution harmony. My developed recommendation has been to manage the thoughts, ideas and the behavior of the personnel placed in charge of procuring the inventory. Without radically changing the current business processes, I introduce some rudimentary systemic visibility modules. These modules link the user to the relative business units in the organization and provide an impact analysis to their individual decisions. By understanding why the cadence of weekly purchases matter to the finance and distribution areas, the business units who write orders quickly spread the receipts and ultimately find better usage of their residual dollars.

Because the typical open to by process was developed to monitor and control monthly activity, the teams never saw the impact of their first of the month ramp up of inventory and lack of receipts in the end of the month. When the efforts of the team are not in synchronization with the objectives, you will continue to see the results of too much, too little, too late and too early on the inventory levels of your organization.

To resolve this dilemma, you need only look into two areas of the company. You will find that the issues reside in either the merchandise buying team and/or your supply chain business unit. The rest of the organization are either supporting the bad habits or enabling them to occur unknowingly. The buying team has one key objective; find what our customers want, pay as little for it as possible and market it at a retail that supports the profitability objectives of the corporation. If you find that they are unfamiliar or don't know what the financial objectives are for their area of responsibility, you've found your problem.   If their knowledge, capabilities and business practices are found to be within reason eighty five percent of the time or greater, the issue is in your supply chain.

Regardless of where the issues are identified, it is the responsibility, *and I'll say it*, the **fiduciary duty** of the executive team to provide guidance and the objectives for a quick and sustainable correction.   While many organizations do not have a resident expert on board who can identify, evaluate and recommend a holistic resolution to your issues, there are plenty of talented consultants that will provide the right answers for your specific issues.

Making Do!

Have you heard this rendition of the truth before?

To produce 10% more sales this year, I will need at least 10% more inventory!

Does it always take more inventory to make more sales? Or, maybe…just maybe it's possible to convert your current levels of inventory with a higher propensity to sell more frequently and with more bottom line results. You may recall my statement in an early chapter that; the amount of inventory is not nearly as important as the content there of. This holds true in all retail activities, the key to a successful revenue and profit campaign is the balance of freshness and brand awareness.

Please don't misinterpret my statement to mean that all you have to do is buy more of the right merchandise and less of the bad. Although that would help tremendously, that is not practical. So what to do? Your success will rely on your reaction to the aligned inventory signals. When your plan has been properly infused with sales and inventory goals, your reaction plans have to regulate the turn objectives. If sales are consistently slower than expected, a modified pricing structure such as promotions or discounts may be in order. Or you may find that the marketing or visuals for the product are falling short of expectations and an inventory flow modification is in order. Whatever the case, the reaction to the numbers on a timely basis is critical.

Before you plant the seed to reduce inventory and increase turns, you have to be aware of the core values of your organization. The reduction of receipts, as good as it may appear on paper, is only a viable option if the you have plenty of what the customer wants today; and you are confident of what they will be looking for tomorrow!

The freshness of your inventory, or put another way, the frequency of receipts is an important component of customer care and developing loyalty. When your inventory becomes stale, tired and shop worn, your ability to command a fair market value for said a commodity is lost. Not only do you jeopardize your sales, you also ultimately jeopardize your brand. Having awareness of who you are to the consumer and being able to capitalize on your strengths while mitigating your weaknesses is what is expected in an effort to reinforce your particular value proposition.

As a first pass to getting to the *right* answers, you only have to gather some readily available statistics. A quick request to your information technology area, or your executive team and you will have a 35,000-foot view of why and how the consumer shops with you.

The request should look something like this:

1. Top 25 selling items for the past (12) months ranked by units. Display the ticketed retail in one column; show the average selling retail in the adjacent column.

    a. This will illustrate the types of items most frequently purchased as well as how much of a discount it takes on average to attract the purchase.

2. The Average 25 selling items for the same time period. Illustrate the same data as the top sellers.

    a. Find the average by taking the total number of units divided by the number of items. At the true average from your ranking, list the 12 items above your average and the 12 items below your average to equal 25 when combined with your average.

3. Finally, take your average that you calculated in step 2 and multiply it by .35 or 35%. This will be your bottom item, from this point count the next 24 earlier ranking items and list the appropriate data.

Now with this data we will accurately surmise who our customer is, when we attract them and how dynamic their tastes are to a changing environment. We will obviously need a few tools to extract the individual characteristics of this data, however the surface information will be unmistakable and relative with a few points of margin error.

From here we can devise a plan, and prepare a process to strategically engage our associates' ability to optimize the current level of inventory. Once you have identified what you SHOULD look like at this inventory level, the proper liquidation strategies can be put into place and a timeline can be constructed to illustrate progress and estimated time of completion.

Chapter 15

Forecasting, What are the ABC's

We have found over the years that our best efforts to infuse great technology, exceptional analysts and layers of planning structures has exasperated our ability to perform a consistent and continual basic forecast. This montage of structures and complicated processes has left many companies asking, what version of the truth are we using to forecast? They have become the statistical arena for conclusions as to what the consumer wants and needs as opposed to a more balanced approach to decision making? How quickly do you react to your indicators and when do you stop buying and take your profits to the bank?

Just as the investment community has long chanted the mantra that "the past results are not an indicator of future direction", so this be the battle cry for retail establishments. The consumer has changed their buying behavior drastically over the past few years. These pattern changes are due in part to the persistent personal economic conditions, and partly due to the strong discounts and marketing tactics being deployed by the retailers. A deeper dive into the raw data and key performance indicators will be necessary to ensure that the actions taken from business indicators will not hinder the prosperity of the organization. Anyone can promote traffic patterns based on promotions, not everyone can do it as a balanced approach to sustained profits.

Forecasts can no longer be relied upon once the demand shifts of the past 2 weeks have been infused. What will ultimately create a good forecast are the combined efforts of the aligned business teams through reactive consistent communications. Each business entity is driven independently to evaluate, rationalize and illustrate their efforts in a timeline. This should include sales, inventory and gross margin assumptions for the upcoming sales period. As the target indicators are then aligned on a graph, an autonomous version of the truth will prevail.

We are now well beyond the single demand forecast that use to control the dynamics of all the adjacent business units. The merchandise area would typically bark out their planned sales, and the rest of the organization would wag their tails. A more complex and integrated process is required today to bring points of concern and financial controls into the resolve. However, these complexities are not the labor elements of the teams making the final decisions. The bulk of the optimization criteria must happen behind the scenes based on the guiding and global business rules. In any economy, the best approach to forecasting is one that is simple, compliant in nature to the resources and assets of your organization, and answers what I call the ABC's of forecasting.

Let me make sure that we get one thing straight and fully understood from the very beginning. The last few years have in no way, shape or form been indicative of a time previous, or a time going forward. The unprecedented events, actions, feelings and outcomes have forever changed the docile landscapes of business and made us all aware of the need for clinical processes and a diligent workforce. Your goal will be to not over complicate the business. It is when the complexities of obtaining your goals overcome the abilities and actions of the assigned teams that generally cause businesses to fail.

During the financial quarters of 2009 through 2011 there were many cracks discovered in the crystal balls of forecasting throughout the retail environment. No matter how you or your team attempted to interpret the historical data, you could not utilize your traditional analysis to accurately predict the future. So some of the more intellectually advanced retailers began using a strategy that applies more credence to the current trends when predictive analytics are driving the forecast.

Rather than relying on the seasonal profiles of the past, the trend was targeted more towards the recovery efforts that dictated the country's emotions, and thus buying habits. The housing market became a key component as well as the financial markets. The financial markets were used more as a component of current trends and the housing market data was used to drive a profile basis. Hope no longer has a place at the forecasting table of discussions. As the feelings for a rapid recovery diminished with time in 2011, so did the exclamation of better performances next year, become a hollow banter.

With such volatility in the retail market and consumers torn between conserving and gratifying their spending pleasure principles, we have to adjust our retail strategies accordingly. With the Federal Reserve aggressively cutting interest rates and many Americans enjoying the windfall of generous price reductions, retailers are prepared to capture as much share of wallet as they can. Many retailers have increased their year over year inventory levels and made unnatural adjustments to their cadence of advertising expenses in pursuit of the bounty bestowed on the general public.

So, how does one forecast such efforts and capitalize on the knowledge of having insider information on the emotions of the country. Statistical models that have performed well in the past are useless today and will need serious modifications to be effective in the future. 2012 will be an election year like no other due to the economy and the characters that are portraying likely candidates. With the political jockeying and sound bites that surround this event getting into full swing, forecasts are going to become even more unreliable. The peaks and valleys of the economy and the affects this will have on the average consumer, define a whole new meaning to riding the waves.

There have been many milestones in recent years to the collection and usage of granular data at the item, store and day level. We now have technology available to us, for the right price, which can illustrate graphically this once impervious collection of multiple statistics. With a few simple mouse clicks you can display a chart or graph depicting every consumer by zip code that has shopped your store and at least one of your competitors in the last week, purchased a pair of jeans at the same time they purchased chewing gum, have 2.4 kids and drive a Toyota that is between 3 and 6 years old.

Now what?

This level of data was to be the promise land; *if we knew these types of differentiators we could harness that power and embrace our consumer directly*…and on and on…

The fact of the matter is we DO have that type of data and we still can't tell what their individual reaction is going to be to some new stimulus that comes out this week...a hurricane, bad employment numbers, another company bankruptcy...etc. Just as the old saying goes; you have little white lies, you have the obligatory out and out horrific lies – and then you have statistics.

That is why just about every retail and business forecast model has an underlying base algorithm called *stochastic* calculations. Which means; that the process involves *guesswork*! That is a piece of complex human behavioral patterns that you cannot and will not master, regardless of how deep you dive into the data. With the economic conditions to remain in turmoil at least until the 2012 elections, the only real forecast that you can believe in is the one that is based on modest fluctuations to the current trends.

Simplify Your Forecasting Methodology

Some planning and financial analyst insist that the current mathematical engines are displaying data that can be accurately evaluated to portray the outcome of shopping habits of your future customers. Those people should be replaced as soon as possible. It is far more important for your company to listen to your current customers and only deviate slightly from their shopping patterns of 6 – 8 weeks ago. Seasonal pattern adjustments will be the most dramatic influences you should allow to be a part of your statistics.

Future growth will come from those who mitigate losses. There is an art to making the right merchandise picks for your customers; there is a science to managing your inventory and profits. The old saying of high-risk will return high-rewards are also the strategy used by gamblers against the house. I don't need to tell you who usually wins that strategic interaction. In today's economy we are the gamblers, and the customers are the houses. So, if we want to survive and thrive beyond 2012 we have to get back to basics in our forecasting.

The three most important rules to remember are;

    A.   Normalize your data.
          a. If the information includes a one time event like a new introduction, non-repeating promotion i.e. grand opening event or special abnormality like weather..i.e. wide spread tornados, hurricane, earthquakes…you will want to smooth these peaks and valleys based on average weekly sales for the similar period.

    B.   Apply a high level calculation against the available inventory on top selling items.
          a. This process aligns a market basket data approach to the selling of remaining products. If you run out of that which brings a majority of your customers in, you will not sell the remaining items as well.

C. Assume flat to no more than a 5% increase for the next 6 – 8 weeks going forward.

   a. On the basis of a downward trend, maintain the same perspective on the negative side. Obviously you will want to adjust your inventory turn assumptions down as you follow a downtrend. Otherwise, eventually it is a self-fulfilling event of obliteration.

The accuracy of your future forecasts will depend greatly on your ability to take the complexities of daily evaluations out of the hands of your associates. A well defined, established and easily managed set of business guidelines and governing principles will suffice as the new rules of engagement for your teams to follow.

Remember to keep it simple and easy to duplicate.

Chapter 16

Finding the Right Software Solution

Today's competitive marketplace has nothing on what it will be like in the upcoming years. The 10-letter word that will enable you to distinguish your company's offerings to your intended audience is, **uniqueness**. How will you and your company navigate the seemingly endless array of software offerings and vendor dominance? Do you go for an ERP System or are you better off approaching from a BOB or Best Of Breed perspective based on your current strengths and weaknesses?

There are quite literally thousands of software offerings out there that promise the world and guarantee that your operations can be optimized through the use of their product. So deciding on the right technology will encompass more than who provided the best presentation or slickest interface. The requirements should be a focused list based on the things you know your company does well, and those where you know you need to do better. Document where you are today, where you were this time two years ago and where you need to be two years from now. Once that list is produced, you can now disseminate it to the different business units, first individual units and later as a collaborative group. You do this so that you can create appropriate dialog with the groups, find their pain points and look for common resolutions.

Throughout the evolution of my career from entry level, to manager, to director, Vice President, Senior Vice President and President, I have worked with a diverse collection of merchandise and types of businesses. I can tell you first hand that the road to prosperity is very much conducive to the types of goals, implementation process roadmaps and training of the technology deployed. To maintain a consistent level of revenue growth during the tough economical times, you more than likely are finding yourself between a rock and a hard place between increased merchandise and operational costs and lower average unit price points out the door.

You will always want to position your organization with the most innovative and scalable technologies. Your outlook should also include the technologies that will enable your team's current and most relevant business processes to be extremely effective. Making sure that any change in processes does not affect the ability to be the type of company your customers believe in. There are far too many canned packages that you can buy off the shelf that are directionally sound, but require more from your teams than they have to offer. One of your key objectives should also center on the goal to mitigate any and all extenuating processes that are in use today that produce little value.

But what's right for your company? The first step is to ensure that your business goals and requirements are articulated and fully rationalized. It isn't a bad business practice to employ an outside entity to interview, document and propose a resolution based on your corporation's input. Knowing that you don't have all the answers let alone experience in dealing with past failures is not an admission of failure. It is an accreditation to knowing what you don't know, and finding the answer. Ultimately your internal leadership team should make the final decision as each business unit has specific needs and wants. As one business unit, lets say marketing, continues to differentiate the products and services offered by your organization, another business unit, this time distribution, is streamlining their staff and making cost cutting changes that negatively impact the fulfillment of promises at store level that marketing has published.

To effectively manage this push / pull on resources, merchandise and goals; you will need to recognize the need for collaboration. To succeed on a consistent basis with as little extenuating effort as possible, all roads must lead to understanding your customer base while anticipating their future demands. To do this properly you must align the needs of your sales data, allocations, buying, pricing, forecast planning, marketing, supply chain and operations channels. The mistake that a lot of organizations make is providing additional data to the user community when additional information is needed.

Data usually emanates in the form of a report from the information that has been deemed as a source. The decision process guidelines usually do not exist in this data report and thus is left to the imagination and ability of the person in possession of the document. The preferred counter is actionable and options based information that is derived from business intelligence. This has been a substantial and fundamental miss that is repeated from the largest organizations to the mom and pop store on the corner.

What you must steer clear of is a situation where a decree is launched from a short-sided evaluation on how to grow sales result. The resolution will often pertain in a process of driving revenue with diminishing profits. When approached with a resolution to infuse a single area with a superior system, stop! There is no way to improve the service level or revenue of an organization without understanding the cause and effect of the entire supply chain and decision making processes within. Increased demand on a supplier that cannot service your needs, or a radical change in the amount of trailers on your distribution center's lot will not bode well for a sustained improvement to your customer's demands.

The best vendors are just as committed to supporting your efforts as they are with the initial sale. You can produce a general assessment by reviewing their ongoing support from a technical as well as phased training efforts. You want a partnership that has its' roots in the process of improving your business. Your laser-focused goal has to be on streamlining the business processes and integrating the decision-making data. This is how you ensure best practices and effective, efficient retail management solutions are ubiquitously adopted. Your company can and will gain a competitive edge with such an implementation now. Having a solid foundation from which to build upon as this economy slowly heals will be the difference between descent growth spurts and sustained compound growth.

The common issue is that today you are faced with a growing number of complexities; from the number of sales channels you must incorporate into a singular view, to the demands from the consumers. With the lightening speed of information and the growing use of web-enabled handsets, your offerings are being researched, reviewed and auctioned to the lowest bidder online. The term *customer loyalty* is quickly becoming an oxymoron. So the challenge has become, how do you cater to a customer that requires instant gratification at a low cost no matter where they are shopping; online, in your store, in your competitor's store. The window of opportunity to persuade that consumer that you are the retailer of choice is small...and it's getting smaller.

"Customers will <u>rarely</u> remember their efforts to find you, they will <u>always</u> remember how you made them feel during the experience." rlt

These times are different

There was a time when retailers would be forced to rely on a canned package from a software solution vendor that produced the best thing since sliced bread. These solutions would require a license and be installed within your current architecture or utilize a stand-alone server. The application would sometimes be referred to as a *best-of-breed* approach. Which was a battle cry that would differentiate a software vendor from the behemoths that were selling Enterprise Resource Planning or ERP systems that would promise to tie all of your disparate systems and processes together in one neat little basket. Most companies found that this was a very expensive initial investment and the ongoing maintenance fees created an unjustifiable expense when the systems would not always be as effective in some areas of the company as they were in others.

Ultimately, the IT resources needed to properly execute the task of integrating your supply chain resources proved to be too expensive for the average retailer. The $500 million and up retailers could afford the best of breed approach and would have the resources and appeal to attract and retain some of the best and brightest managers available. This created an opportunity for some sharp software vendors who could produce retail technology that would be cost effective and simple to execute with reasonable return on investment expectations for the small and medium-sized retailers.

Today you would be well advised to pursue a software solution from a vendor who can provide your company with a high degree of technology that is scalable, consumer centric, best or breed single application. The processes to operate should be seamless to your business units and collaborative real-time responses across your key areas. A good strategic partner will enable your operations to react as efficiently and effectively as your big-box counterparts, but with costs conducive and sensitive to your budget and needs.

Because the cross-channel retail complexity of yesterday will only become more intensified in the future, you will want a solution that can assemble your customer purchases from all avenues into a single version of total sales. The visibility of the separate transactions will only be necessary, as the evaluation of growth channels becomes a needed analysis. The freedom demanded by your customers to shop when, where and how they wish cannot be controlled by your inflexible systems or processes. Like running water, the path to another retailer will be their choice if they find resistance from you to accommodate their current needs.

Consumer Centric Demand patterns is more than just a term of process engineering. It should be the foundation by which each of your business units derives their day-to-day activities. Understanding the need to be serviced quickly, effectively and then personally thanked for their patronage will help drive your business model and thus software solution requirements. With this foundation you will be better equipped to derive the right assortments, at the right time, for the diverse consumer shopping habits at each of your locations. You will then be equipped to easily identify the price points that inspire multiple purchases and frequent shopping trips.

Who's the best?

There are a lot of options out there for you to choose from when it comes to deploying software. The best retail business software solution is the one that has the resources, time and expertise to resolve your top 5 issues as designated by your executive steering committee within the budgetary constraints. The best practice in this area is to put together a requirement sheet that illustrates the top issues, what systems you have today, who currently is responsible for resolving the issues and the basis of your resolution ideas.

Send this requirement sheet to a minimum of 5 vendors, you can find these vendors through a simple Google search or via a trade publication or show. Be leery of those vendors who respond back to you with EXTRA things…they are looking for a larger sale and disregard the fact that you have already listed your requirements as;

Fundamental, and Resource Influenced to negate the EXTRAS.

Remember,

"even if you have the fastest car on the racetrack, you are not going to win many races unless you have well-qualified and astute drivers". rlt

In other words, be sure the vendor's technology fits the business acumen of your user community. You do not want to water down a system, and yet you don't want the pure numbers to be the ultimate way you run your business. When in doubt you should always resort to asking for guidance, not solutions. The issues perplexing your organization may be globally the same as others, but the intricacy needed to properly deal with them in your company will always be different. When the directions are obeyed and adhered to by the letter, following the same path does not automatically equate to achieving the same results. The devil is in the detail, and the detail must be fully understood.

Chapter 17

Why Benchmarking Has Failed

Are we as good as we should be? How do we compare to others in our market place? Can we continue to grow at this rate without additional labor costs? These are the quintessential question for all retailers and businesses alike. Since the beginning of retail times there have been charts and graphs and statistics that provided value or concern to leaders in the form of a benchmark review. This dubious and often considered a biblical report depicts your corporation's efforts against those in your category. The established common evaluations began with monthly and annual sales. Then it progressed to sales per square foot to offer a more cleansed review and began the adaptation of the performance standards.

And there my friend is where the practice of benchmarking took a turn for the worse. When the efforts of like organizations, by the sheer aggregate of growth, took very different conceptual approaches to the reporting of common data. Just as the differences that make a company appeal to their customer base, such differences can impact the qualitative comparisons on statistical data. It comes down to the governing body of the statistics and how those who wish to know interpret them.

The main issue is that for most businesses the very existence of a benchmark conjures up notions of necessity over nicety.   What began as a common practice self improvement tool for businesses to utilize as a measuring stick to one another, quickly became a competitive arena. Just as we have found that rarely is there anything common about common sense in today's society, so is there a substantial variance in standards when it comes to the evaluation of performance standards. You rarely will find an exact apple to apples evaluation from the governing bodies in retail.   There are inherent differences in the classification of the sales and profits, inventory and timing.

Some of the companies use a FIFO or first in first out evaluation of their assets, while others use an average at cost against a hypothetical markup to obtain a retail standard. Then you have the cutoff variances to when the snapshot data is taken. Some use a quarterly snapshot while others illustrate a run rate equal to the time of the request. All in all you have distinct variances aligned in a document that is now being utilized to plot strategies and create symmetry where none exists.

There isn't anyone within the retail community who doesn't like to be judged on his or her own scale of curriculum. However, there is no practical or financial relevance to beating your competition if their trajectory is not on par with who you are trying to be. That is why so much emphasis has been put on retail performance standards and objectives. To validate these objectives each company looks towards the leaders within their genre of merchandise offerings and channel of business.

So what has gone wrong? Why is it no longer relevant to place your cards on the table against your closest or most admired competitor and measure them in an honest and objective manner?

The answer can be found in the approach to finding the reality why your company is in the race for customers in the first place. Over the years of benchmarking our best practices and formulating strategies along parallel fences with your competition, you have become your competition. While your goal was to mimic what you thought was the right refection cast by your competitor, you were in a sense following their lead. It happened so gradually that you may not have noticed that there isn't a lot of differentiation between you and your competitors…that is… if you listen to your customers. You personally may be able to rattle off fifteen separate ways that you differentiate yourself from your competition, but your objective opinion isn't how the customer sees things.

To obtain the truth, assuming you CAN handle the truth, you have to know what your customers *need* from you the majority of the time, and just as important, what they *want* from you on a consistent basis. Their needs and wants are your commands. Anything less and you are destined to be another historical retailer that just didn't get it. CCR has to become commonplace within your companies everyday jargon and business practices. No, not Creedence Clearwater Revival…now you're really showing your age…I'm talking about **Collaborative Customer Relationships**. A recent study showed that more than **63%** of shoppers are emotionally motivated to make purchases. *Personally, I think that number is much higher, more like 80+%.* They look for gratification after their purchase decisions and want to enjoy that moment again and again. Many retailers have mistakenly interpreted this to mean simple price reductions or savings. Although these stimuli are gratifying to the consumer, what they really want is to be recognized, admired, talked to, nurtured, respected and thanked.

After all, this is a long tem relationship you are trying to establish not a chance encounter. Sorry guys, right now I am speaking to the ladies. Have you had this conversation, or at least thought of having this conversation with your significant other recently? What stopped you? Ah yes, you didn't think they would listen or that they just wouldn't understand what are your true needs.

Hmm…and most retail organizations are male dominated. Hello? Is anyone getting a correlation here?

Remember, only 37% of the population truly gets the numbers game that we have been using so vigorously in our media and store signage campaigns since our $450 billion dollar Bentonville gorilla in the room was a 3-store chain with aspirations.

Who among us will be the first to transcend this holy grail of retail?

What do you do if you can't show sale prices, percentages off, clearance, markdowns and the like?   How about reaching out from the store shelves with talking points? I'm not referring to the big red starbursts with yellow lettering or the *As Advertised, price drop* or *clearance* blips all over your store today. What is wrong with?:

Hello, I'm on sale today! or *I'm Sorry, this is sold out.*

Please touch the red button above to help us record your needs…we'll do better next time with your help!

That may be too much for a shelf talker, but you get my message. Treat them with empathy and understanding that they have choices to make everyday and today they chose to shop with you, don't let a missed sale turn into a lost customer.

Tailor your business objectives and expectations to your consumer

Don't try to make your *round* company fit into a *square* comparison. When approaching the best of breed practices of your competition, be sure that you allow for differentiation of customers and commodity. This will ensure that your approach to benchmarking has relevance and your quantitative analysis will support the decision-making processes for qualitative changes in the future. When you make direct comparisons between your business and your closest competitors, you should be looking for differentiators and not ways to mimic their behaviors. To sustain growth and profitability there is a host of strengths and weakness that will have to be addressed in relation to your chosen path as a retailer. To gain powerful insight to build your organization from a solid foundation, you must engage expertise and experience. Too often retailers pull the proverbial trigger on a new direction without fully understanding the risk/reward quotient and thus become overwhelmed with the negative supply chain responses to this new catalyst.

Chapter 18

Service Level Optimization

Whenever your company embarks upon a campaign to optimize their inventory and procurement processes, and believe me...if you haven't done so in the past six months to a year...you will. You can rest assured that your team will commit at least one of the three major and consistent mistakes made by the executive teams in retail.

1. The resolution focus will be myopic in nature, concentrating on the issues at hand today and not on the root causes or the future.

2. The wrong person or people will be placed in charge of piloting the project.

3. Or last, but certainly not least, the budget will not support the goals and standards established as objectives for the project.

When surveying the project expectations with the real costs of the project, you will want to be comfortable with the timeline and resources needed. Many organizers fail to relate their real costs to acquire and serve their customers with the profitability requirements per each category of merchandise offerings. Someone on your steering committee team must understand your working capital requirements to obtain a relational understanding of your gross margin and return on investment objectives.

There are a multitude of examples in the retailer's graveyard where the execution of a process was flawless and the right system was implemented and yet, the results were a disaster. Although many reasons exist as to why they failed in their quest for retail dominance and effective and efficient process, they can usually be found within these areas.

- Poorly regulated supply chain activity from end to end. Knowing your optimum service level based on the cost, margin, pipeline capacity, lead time variables and symbiotic process constraints.

- Lack of consumer centric demand patterned assortment rationalization. Keeping the right goods in front of YOUR key customers by individual location demographics.

- Truly understanding space performance measurements and the impact of change on the dollars per square foot analysis.

Service level optimization is not a single sided project as many vendors may proclaim. The models usually presented lack the conditional aspect variables to deal with the unenviable task of increasing customer satisfaction. The sellers will proclaim that it is in there, but where is the dashboard that illustrates the past, present and future conditions in a simple, easy to understand interface? All controllable business units have to be engaged not just the initial user community.

As you begin to understand that to be in-stock on a commodity is not the same as having an acceptable service level. It's like saying that you have gas in your tank and not knowing how far you can get with the amount of gas you have. Many factors create a conditional response like the terrain you'll be driving and the efficiencies of your engine. If you once believed that an in stock and a service level where indeed interchangeable, you were not alone. Let me be the one who clears this myth up for you once and for all. You will find that most retailers interchange the term In-stocks and service levels based on an old wise tale that each term describes an amount of inventory. The term In-stock refers to a state of inventory at a particular time in a particular location and cannot be quantitatively linked to a degree of customer satisfaction.

Service level, on the other hand has a direct and mathematically sustained correlation to customer satisfaction by illustrating numerically how many consumers will/would be ringing the registers with their purchase of said commodity before the inventory runs out. A quick rule of thumb to help you remember these terms are that one unit on the shelf constitutes an in-stock of 100%. That same one unit, which has an average weekly sales velocity of four units, has a 25% service level. Simply stated, you will disappoint three customers that week due to being out of stock.

How do we get our service levels optimized?

Now that we have a more formal understanding of the composition of service levels, let's discuss how we will optimize the service levels of your organization. The key to establishing your goals is to first understand where you are today, what issues are causing the greatest delineation to your goal, what the true costs are and what resources are needed to achieve and maintain the new objective.

Another common mistake made by the general retail population when they set out to achieve optimization of their service levels is the rationalization, or lack there of, of their current assortment offerings to their customers. Just as important as having the merchandise available, it behooves the retailer to have the *__right__* merchandise to sell. This mistake can almost always be linked back to the cause for failure in achieving the initial goals. The costs are generally prohibitive when you blindly increase a service level requirement ubiquitously without understanding the end-to-end impact on the corporation.

Because service levels impact your inventory levels, this is the first place that has to be understood and rationalized at a high level. To begin your strategy, understand that a properly rationalized assortment will produce between (40 – 60) points of improvement to your turn. Remember my *Basic Rule of Fifty*; 25% percent of your items are exceedingly below your optimization level of service, meaning they are selling too fast. 50% of them are within a tolerable margin of error to your goal, and 25% of them are egregiously overstocked to their sales and return on inventory investment. Thus you produce a campaign to work on the top and bottom 25% each area, and allow the middle 50% to maintain while the payback efforts ensue on the two extreme ends.

Once you've identified the items that encompass the basic rule of fifty, you now need to establish the rules of engagement to rationalizing and setting your inventory goals. To keep it simple, lets assume that you have $1 million dollars of average inventory and you have a current turn of 2.00 annually. Utilizing my factors, you will be able to increase your turn to 2.40 – 2.60 without increasing your inventory. You will decrease your overall inventory by 10% and increase sales by 8%.

The numbers look like this; **prior** to optimization you were selling $2 million annually with $1 million in average inventory. **Post** optimization, you will produce $2.16 million on an inventory base of $900 thousand. This minimum combination of focused sales and rationalized inventory results in a 2.40 inventory turn. All of this with an improved service level that identifies the best selling, most profitable consumer centric merchandise and places it in the right stores, more frequently with minimal warehouse occupation.

Optimization and affordability have to be tantamount when discussing the stages of system and process implementation. If I need one million dollars of average inventory to sustain my service level goal, and my cash reserves are at critical mass at the eight hundred thousand mark, you're not optimized.

Chapter 19

The Daily Grind
(Part: 3 of 3)

When systems fail to deliver the agreed upon expectations or results, it's considered technical difficulties in your digital information systems area, a fix is implemented and life goes on. When people fail to deliver the agreed upon expectations or results, it's considered *reasons for dismissal* and the institution can no longer survive under these conditions. Someone gets fired! No doubt you've heard the term that your actions speak louder than words. Well I am here to help you understand that sometimes your words can far exceed your actions.

It was not the best of times for the company and everyone was feeling the pressure. Even the most minuscule of issues gets blown out of proportion during these times because most executives fail to set precedence. When the leaders truly lead, the rest will follow willingly and without hesitation.

"What the heck is going on?" Norman asks in a frantic voice.

"I just heard that Mark Jacobs quit!" Says Linda Weismann a star senior planner for the company for the past ten years.

"Not quit. FIRED"! Said Mike Thompson in a solemn voice as he carefully views the manicure on his right hand.

"Fired? You've got to be kidding me; he's been here for over 15 years. This was only the second job he ever had in his professional life."

Norman was especially upset because he and Mark went to lunch every Thursday like clockwork. They had begun the ritual during a project to introduce price optimization into the company 5 years ago and just continued it up until this past Thursday.

"What's the story?" Norman asks, knowing that he is probably going to get just that, a story, full of embellishments and enhancements because…well, that's Mike.

"He was found to be insubordinate to Mr. Trent when Mark was asked why his area was constantly losing sales and profits for the past 6 months." Mike says in a monotone voice.

"What in God's name did Mark say to that?" Norman asks in a half grinning, half grimacing face.

"He said he didn't know."

"He got fired for saying he didn't know?" Norman placed the palm of his left hand on his forehead and began to rub gently back and forth as he peered at his shoes.

"That just doesn't sound like grounds for dismissal to me."

"You didn't let me finish." Mike announced as he rolled his eyes and turned his head towards the door on the side.

"Mark looks up at Mr. Trent and says in a condescending voice, do *you* know why my sales and profits have been declining for the last 6 months Mr. Trent?"

"OMG!   Tell me you're kidding!" Norman says as he doubles over as if someone hit him in the stomach.

"I was in the meeting." Mike says "and you could have heard a pin drop after Mark's question."

"The next thing we heard was Mr. Trent saying; *the rest of you are dismissed, thank you for your efforts and keep up the hard work.*"

"I was the last one out and I tried to get eye contact with Mark when Mr. Trent looks right at me and says; please close the door Mike."

"About an hour later we hear a page for Jamie Craoughton to come to Mr. Trent's office immediately."

Jamie is the head of human resources and is usually not paged because she is in her office working her magic on benefits, insurance premium reductions and many other thankless tasks that she is so brilliant with.

"That's when I knew it was all over for Mark!" Mike delivers his infamous rendition of an umpire calling a player OUT! in a big league game.

Norman neglects to find the humor in the portrayal of the situation by Mike. Regardless of how you felt about Mark, he was a 50+ year old veteran of this organization and up until these past few years, was a positive contributor to this corporation's top and bottom line. Hell, Mark won the buyer of the year award back to back in 2007 and 2008!

"He hasn't left the building yet has he?" Norman asks.

"Yep! Security escorted him out with a small box of his most valued possessions and they will arrange for him to come back in Saturday morning to get the rest of his belongings." Mike states in a matter of fact tone and facial expressions.

"I know this because I cornered Jamie in her office and got the scoop while it was hot!" Mike leans back in his chair and says;

"I have first dibs on his office."

Rather than to fulfill his fantasy of jumping over the desk and tightly clasping both hands around Mike's neck while chanting – *shut up, shut up, shut up*…. Norman composes himself, smiles and turns to head back to his office.

Over his shoulder he peers at Mike and says;

"You haven't exactly blown your numbers out of the water the past couple of months…and I noticed one of the newbies measuring your office yesterday."

Norman continues to walk away and hears Mike's reply,

"Bullshit, you're out of your mind!"

Mike jumps to his feet and stops at his doorway.

"Which one of the newbies was in here Norman?"

"Norman?"

"Let me catch the son-of-a-b**** in my office!"

At than moment Mike feels the eerie gaze of eyes and resentment from everyone in a 20-foot radius that is now starring at him in disbelief.

"What are you look'en at? Don't you have work to do?" he spouts off

Mike turns and slams his door as if what Norman had just said to him had a shred of truth to it.

Although, when you look at them, Mike's numbers really haven't been up to par lately.

Next-Day

It had all of the great hallmarks of being a typical Friday, fewer cars in the parking lot, less people doing the quick step through the glass double door entry into the security area, and at least two empty spots where the executives park. The weatherman called for clear blue skies and a high temperature of 77 degrees. As Norman peered at the names on the posts where the two executives' cars would normally have obstructed such a view, he rubbed his chin and thought;

"I wonder when their Golf tee time is this morning?"
Norman looks up into the radiant blue sky and thinks to himself,

Oh well, at least I don't have to sweat out that report they said they needed – *FIRST THING FRIDAY MORNING!!*

Yesterday, that report was made out to be the saving grace of the entire third quarter and without that data, we might as well kiss our bonus potential good-bye. Funny how a warm fall day and available tee times at the local golf range changes the perspective. Not to look a gift horse in the mouth, Norman proceeds towards the double doors with his access badge in hand.

"Good morning Jennifer!" Norm blares out from behind his desk with his eyes focused on the reports in front of him as he sits down.

No response. However that doesn't get Norman's attention, the sound of Jennifer's conversation on the phone quickly resolves any concerns over her not reciprocating the greeting.

He can't help but to over hear some of her conversation;

"I know, but why would they keep her and let him go?"

"Oh, please…. are you serious?"

"Well if that happens, I'm outta here!"

"O.K., Norman just walked in so I gotta go, call me if you hear anything else."

With that Jennifer hangs up the phone, slowly stands, grabs a writing tablet and heads towards Norman's office.

Norman is seeing all of this through peripheral vision as he pretends to be studying a report. He is moving his lips in cadence to the written words as he glides his fingers over each word and number; pretending as if he needs to memorize it for a meeting.

Jennifer quick steps into his office, grabs the doorknob and asks; "do you mind if I close this?"

As she pulls the door towards her and then yanks it closed.

"Have you heard?" Jennifer asks in a wide-eyed forward crouching motion that ends in the chair in front of Norman's desk.

"Heard what?" Norman says in a (*I have no idea*) voice.

"Mr. Crocker is gone!" Jennifer says cocking her head to one side and flipping her thumb like a baseball umpire calling the final strike.

"What?" "When?" "Why?"

Norman's succession of questions come from a unique area of the human psyche. You see, Mr. Crocker was one of the so called; *dynamic duo* of the company who's car was not parked in its normal spot. Norman isn't the type of person who dislikes too many people. But Mr. Crocker was bound and determined to be one of those people. No one knew that Norman had an aversion   for Mr. Crocker because he just didn't talk about people and certainly not his superiors. So the news was bitter sweet to Norman, bitter because he never wished ill will on anyone; and sweet because he no longer has to deal with unrelenting requests for answers to questions that do not make a difference in tomorrow's decisions.

"Well, Michelle was just telling me that Mr. Trent called Mr. Crocker into his office around 7:45 a.m."

"She said that when Mr. Crocker arrived, she knocked and then opened Mr. Trent's door and announced that Mr. Crocker was here."

Then he uttered those four solemn and ever telling words, *please close the door* and she knows from experience what was about to happen.

After about 20 minutes of garbled words from each of them, Mr. Crocker left the office with his head down and a scowl on his face.

As Jennifer meticulously recalled the chain of events, Norman leaned further and further back into his chair as though he was captivated by the story. Not saying a word, but providing ample body language and facial contortions to appease Jennifer's thirst for acceptance as the messenger.

"Then after Crocker left, Mr. Trent asked Michelle to get security on his line." Jennifer stated matter of factly as she raised her chin to the air and widened her eyes.

"Michelle said that she heard him say to security; I need an escort sent to Mr. Crocker's office, he is no longer an associate of this company."

Jennifer falls back into the seat after delivering that speech as if she was completely spent.

"Does Michelle know why he was let go?" Norman asks as if it would make a difference.

Jennifer perks back up after catching her second wind!

"Rumor has it that Mr. Crocker was on probation for actively trading some of his restricted shares on the open market without discussing the sale with the CFO. But that was like a year ago."

Jennifer looks quickly down at the ground, and then back up to Norman.
"Can they do that?"

Norman tilts his head and gives a half smile.

"Oh yes, the Feds probably took this long to accumulate the evidence and proper documentation. If that is indeed the reason, we will hear a whole lot more about this as the SEC gets their piece of him."

Norman catches himself. He composes his emotions and remembers that this man's life, family and potential future are in jeopardy and no one should speak in a disrespectful manner.

"Well, I hope that for his family's sake he can continue to provide for them and ensure a future void of despair and angst."

With that, Jennifer rises to her feet, adorns a warm smile and looks into the direction of Norman and says;

"You really are good people Norman."

She turns to the door and says as if she forgot something.

"Oh, by the way…. Good Morning!"

BUSINESS AS USUAL

It was 4:15 p.m. on a Wednesday before the scheduled Thursday morning quarterly board of director's meeting. The executives were all pretty exhausted because finally, after the eighth revision of their capital expenses, labor estimates and inventory assumptions they had an initial sales plan to present to the board.   As usual, they congregated in the boardroom with their individual piles of data, analysis and aspirin.

There were a few new faces in the room this quarter, two of them were replacements for those who had fallen to circumstances, or ran for sanctity before them, and one of them a newly created position. For the four members that had weathered the previous storms and knew the drill, they attempted to enlighten their new colleagues as to the expectations and protocol of the next 4 -5 hours. Just as someone was about to interject on a statement referring to reverse logistics initiated by the Chief Operations Officer, the side door was abruptly flung open.

"Can someone give me a hand here?" the CFO, Terry Beach muddled as he kicked open the door and spoke with a pencil suspended between his teeth. His arms were full of drifting books, papers and binders that appeared to be struggling to find their way from his grasp to the floor as he gyrated and twitched in attempted to thwart their efforts.

"Here, let me help you with that." uttered one of the most recent members to the team, James Fenomca.

"Thank you James. Looks like we have a TRUE gentlemen among this Riff-Raff." Terry said loudly and in the direction of the four tenured executives.

James was their newest victim, or more appropriately titled, Senior Vice President of merchandising. He's a tall man, around six foot four or so, with a lean lanky frame that was athletic in stature, accompanied by an awkward gate when he walked.

"What _is_ all of this?" James asked in a partial diaphragm laugh as he removed half of an armful of papers from Terry's right arm.

"You really don't want to know, trust me on this one." Jerry grumbled as he shook his head to and fro. Just then Jerry's eyes suddenly widened as he patrolled the attendants at the executive table.

"Where is William Trent?" Jerry asked in a calm but firm voice.

"He's in the men's room Jerry, let the man take a piss will ya?" jokes Rickie Starnes the COO.

The group chuckles, making sure that Jerry was finding humor in the statement. Rickie isn't always the best at determining the right things to say at the right moment. In fact, he's been known to make an embarrassing statement and being called out on it by the CEO in front of half the company. But that's Rickie, one of the most intelligent people in the realm of his domain. When you get him out of his area of expertise, it's like taking a bull into the china shop. You can't control him, he's going to break something and you prey that the damage can be contained.

"I needed to verify a couple of his numbers before we get started and more importantly..." Terry glances over his right shoulder towards the side door he entered through and lowers his voice to a whisper; "...before Jason gets in here."

Jason Michaels is the Chairman of the board, Chief Executive Officer and founder of the organization. It was he who single handedly guided the organization through the most formidable economic times and pulled off the most brilliant display of retail ingenuity then and since.

At least that's what he continues to tell all those who have the unmitigated gall to infer that they may have more knowledge than he in a particular subject of retail. Matching wits with Jason is a rare feat in itself; considering the academic and business self-indulgence that is performed by him in the majority of the meetings. Most of the time Jason is so preoccupied with proving others wrong, that he sometimes misses an opportunity to remind everyone of, *"...the (3) three things I did to make the difference between surviving and thriving..."*

When he started the meetings off with that statement, you could do nothing but sit back and allow the tale to be told. Three things, always three things, the man is the holy trinity of resolutions and pontification. But for all the flack we bestowed upon him in our separate meetings and lunch tables, the man knew his stuff. There were none better in evaluating financial moves that would keep the organization in front of the investment community and largest shareholders. For all that he is, he is **not** an ignorant man. He may not know as much as he thinks he does, but what he does know is most of the time relevant and on point.

"Would you like me to check on Mr. Trent?" ask one of the other new faces, Gail Shore.

"No Gail, thank you but I don't think it would be appropriate for you to go into the men's room or knock outside the door."

A quick smile came to Terry's face as if he just completed

the best punch line since Johnny Carson.

"I had not intended to …"

Gail's defense statement is interrupted by the belly laughs of the typical males in the room. Today's acceptance of female executive associates has flourished, however the mentality of the "juvenile boys club" has shown little progress when it comes to crass jokes.

"We'll wait a few more minutes before we send a posse out for him." Terry utters as he attempts to contain his laughter.

"Well, speak of the devil."

In walks William Trent right at that moment and although Jerry doesn't admit it, his shoulders relax and a calmness falls over his chubby cheeked face.

"It is so nice of you to join us this evening William." Terry states sarcastically.

"Nice to be appreciated Terry, I'm feeling the love."

William is not an easy target. When you present your offensive line in his direction, you had better be ready for a most formidable defensive play right back. However, most of the time William spends his efforts on finding more efficient and better technological processes to supply information quicker and more accurately to the associates

He's a stern believer that if you communicate openly with your teams, provides them with the best tools possible and makes the time to listen to their issues; they will remain protective of the company and all that you entrust to them.

He's a true leader to be followed.

Chapter 20

Price Optimization
What the market will bear

The industry has spoken, and the key objective being deployed towards retail survival is price optimization. These are two simple words that invoke a sense of rational behavior and recognition that each market has pricing opportunities. The retail rub, as we like to refer this to, is the proper execution of this project. Ownership of a product does not constitute success. How do you implement and maximize the performance of your company without adding additional layers of associates? If done correctly, you won't avoid adding personnel to this area. However, the most recent industry studies have shown a conservative 11 – 14 percent gain in operating profit by being marginally good at pricing effectiveness by one percentage point. Using these statistics as a target, you can quickly value the return on the 2 - 3 associates you'll need to initiate and optimize your endeavor.

The depths by which you will delve into this strategy will depend greatly on your current, and what is more important your future pricing strategy. If you are a high / low operation, meaning you bank on illustrating savings to the customer via off retail. Then you will find that your promotional cadence, geographic zone alignments and competitive business rules will play a much more important factor than if you have unique products or a majority of house brands.

The buying and planning teams will be an instrumental resource in determining a market-based strategy. You will wish to validate these assumptions with more science-based tools that can weed through massive amounts of consumer data for the TRUTH. If you supply the RIGHT players, you will first recognize that all the answers are NOT in the data. Here is a cautionary note: If a vendor selling the latest version of pricing optimization technology approaches you with a claim that it can remove the human intervention...run. There is no substitute for the collaboration of art and science when it comes to pricing optimization.

The most useful, and successful pricing optimization models available today recognize that there must be a symbiotic relationship between the data, the users and your corporation's future objectives. Too many organizations attempt to operate this business unit as a service level, or information-gathering base. This dramatically dilutes the effectiveness and potential of the pricing optimization efforts. Much like a purchase order, the value comes BEFORE it is written. Such is true wherein the value of price optimization comes into play best before the retail price is established. Changing pricing is an expensive and labor-intensive endeavor. Analyze twice, execute once.

The more relevant historical data inputs that can be aligned with the business strategies of the merchandise executives, the more successful the outcome. To achieve utopia in this campaign your strategy will increase overall volume and profits without sacrificing who you are as a company and what the consumer believes to be true about your promotions. You can't advertise 50% off an inflated $2 item to illustrate value when the known market price is $.69. Separating your value proposition by category of merchandise is a key factor when initiating your rules of engagement. The measurement of pricing variance within your categories will assist in your determination of strategies.

I recommend a market basket data approach from the perspective of grouping and classifying your average selling retails per unit. This unique perspective will become a guiding piece of your value argument when separating the coffee maker category into price classifications. The basic premise of this process is to align your selling strategies by putting the higher margin, slower selling $75 - $90 coffee makers in a segregated bucket outside of the $19 - $35 high velocity, low margin items. *More on this subject of price adapted categorization and the proper models to handle the expected impacts to come.*

Knowing *what the market will bear* for your specialized commodity is part of the art within the merchandising area. Understanding the deviation on the mean in a specific geographic area is the science. For years store operations personnel have been perplexed why an item that they can't get enough of is marked down and put into clearance by "the smart people" in the corporation. Ubiquitous pricing strategies, which were all the rage when the Internet selling campaigns began, caused this issue and will cripple a lot of organizations. The key to survival is to fully understand and recognize the power of zone or differential pricing in your individual stores as well as their online businesses.

Today your more progressive organizations have the ability to price by areas of the country and even differentiate their promotional pricing as well.   You need the help of some sophisticated technology to ensure that your competitive market share doesn't lose ground to your zest for margin. Think about having software that was proactive to the Detroit scenario of 2009.   Or one that would surely have predicted the demise of the strategy to illustrate what day your markdowns would occur and to what price point right on the ticket. What got you here, won't keep you here and change will take place with or without you.

If you had stores or a business catering to the public in an affluent area of Detroit in 2009, and that affluence was based on the automotive industry, you were about to see unprecedented rapid changes.

Price optimization tools would have detected the slightest changes but would not have responded until a pattern appeared and then would recommend adjustments to your pricing.   It would not have necessarily invoked a conditional alert would have illustrated that along side the consumer's economic pullback in those areas.   At some point you would have even taken those signals to advance operational floor changes and promotional messages had you not known the macroeconomics that were at play here. Again, when done correctly with the right staff and education of personnel in the pricing optimization area, you will reap the benefits today and more advantageously tomorrow. Now you know me well enough now to know that I am the first to say; all that glitters, is not gold! Pricing optimization is in that arena for sure. This is a very large undertaking for any organization and it takes on a whole different dimension when you have tens and even hundreds of thousands of convoluted items. Not to mention the complexity of working with numerous price zones, the ever-changing costs of commodities, margin goals, and the all too common bottom line improvement *counter strategies* being implemented in adjacent business units.

For instance, when distribution changes the routing of their fleet to accommodate more stores and the backhaul opportunity with vendor ABC is gone, you freight cost will hit the margin line of the items you use to piggyback to your warehouse. One business unit strategy for savings, counters the pricing optimization strategy for those items. It would be humanly impossible and highly irresponsible for an organization to rely on sustaining optimized standards without an investment in technology and the right personnel. When truly optimizing your prices you will be looking for the impact on adjacent items and the classification impact as a whole. You cannot change prices in a vacuum and be effective long-term. A tremendous amount of variables need to be rationalized and complex evaluations need to take place so that your decisions can be executed quickly and measured for effectiveness. Ultimately the process MUST support who you are as a company. You will pay the price for random process changes that impact the customer's impression of what you mean to them. A word of advice; PUT YOUR CUSTOMERS FIRST, do not change for the sake of changing!

That doesn't just mean those customers who ring your registers; it also means those customers who are your suppliers, distribution and store operation business units are also customers in a sense. The impact of a price change can be debilitating to the workforce when the physical pricing must be changed on each item. When you request changes to one flavor or color of a particular item, and the residual flavors or colors remain, you create confusion and resentment of your process.

This can be easily eliminated by communicating your intentions along with the reasons and by requesting a physical move of the single item price change as you would on a clearance request. Otherwise your process assumes that someone knows that the price change is for just one of a group of similar items. Don't rely on *someone*; rely on technology, procedures and communication. The very best technology is one that you introduce because it enables your developed policies and procedures to seamlessly unite the disparate business units of your organization. Price optimization and modeling solutions can provide you with a competitive edge for price and promotion management. Especially when you can compliment them with well thought out business strategies and the right personnel to execute those strategies. Begin with best practices for your organization's goals and objectives.

Keep your focus on your customers and your sensitivity on your team members. The new world of retail is waiting for leaders, what was once the practices of few are now the laws for profitable sustained existence. Without the implementation of robust technology and the right drivers of your strategy, you will be costing your company sales, margin and consumer confidence. In the end, you will want to find the balance between price sensitivity within your category offerings and the profits needed for your organization to survive in this highly competitive arena we call -**RETAIL**-.

Chapter 21
~~~~~~~

Distribution Center Versus Warehouse

Distribution Centers for years have been confused with Warehouses by the general public, as well as executive leaders. The two are truly not synonymous. Although the physical structures will mostly resemble one another, the operational factors of your merchandise procurement processes and more pointedly, your consistent flow of goods are the true differentiators. Distribution centers are commonly known as D.C.'s and are commonly defined as the foundation of a supply chain network. The capacity, location and operational costs, when analyzed properly, will dictate the optimal use of the facility as either a true distribution center or warehouse, and for some more advanced transportation savvy business units they may use part of a facility as a de-consolidation center. However, for this discussion I want to concentrate on factors related to distribution centers and warehouses. Let's take a quick minute and define the two.

A distribution center is operated in a manner where the majority of the goods that are received into the facility have a turn-a-round or shipping window of less than 30 days. If merchandise is received and stored for more than 60 days, using a FIFO, *First In First Out*, methodology of shipping;

then your facility is more aptly described as a warehouse or storage facility. There are times when storage makes sense to a corporation. Known increases in future costs of key items, a special buy offered by vendors, pre-build for promotions or staggered seasonal receipts to name just a few. Just because you store some of the exampled items for more than 60 days does not automatically convert your distribution center to a warehouse. The rule of thumb is if 30% or more of your facility is dedicated to the aforementioned best practices, you are operating in the warehouse capacity. It isn't necessarily a bad thing to have storage associated with your merchandise. It is just common knowledge, and widely adopted to operate under the distribution center model. Your primary objective should always be to keep as much of your merchandise as possible flowing closer to time of need. By doing so you enhance the corporation's ability to receive life-sustaining revenue from sales on merchandise before the vendor's invoice arrives in accounting.

The most practical business model that generates the most successful retail operations is a vendor to store shipping operation on key items. This provides a powerful margin enhancing process by eliminating the handling and resource costs on your corporation's expense line and transferring a portion to added vendor costs. The term for this is Vendor Managed Inventory or VMI for short. We will get into the detailed structure of this model and what controls are needed to regulate the vendor managed inventory agreements in another book. Believe me when I tell you that there is much more to this practice than just "set it, and forget it". Many failed ventures happened because the cart was placed before the horse and no one bothered to recognize the prominent issues. Some have even ventured into this arena without having a strategic plan that answers the questions; what will be the benchmarks of success, and what is the process for change when the statistics illustrate a degradation of the assumptions?

The inventory turn objectives of your corporation, in conjunction with vendor minimums and lead times, combine to establish the rules of engagement as to whether you maintain a distribution center, or warehouse. Ultimately you'll find the right course by analyzing the consumer demand patterns from your store shelves, web, catalog and/or mail order offerings. This information will help to formulate your best plan to control inventory and capitalize on the objective of reducing your carrying costs and physical needs to store merchandise in your supply chain. Most corporations look at their inventory as a pure cost function of doing business. What if instead it was viewed as an asset to accomplishing revenue goals? This small behavioral change can provide a lasting impact on the future rationalizations. Your time and effort would be spent on managing the flow of the product and diverting the conversations and focus on the controlling of the overall quantity. It has been proven, time and time again, that when you make substantial reductions in inventory, the sales rate is soon to follow. Academics and financial gurus alike don't hesitate to illustrate the inefficiencies of certain items during an evaluation of your inventory levels. Many times this one-sided analysis is done without regards to the relational affect the items have on adjacent or comparable merchandise.

I once had a client that ruled the removal of 15% of the items that did not perform to a standard that mathematically and economically made sense. But the missing link that I uncovered was that the information provided was not evaluated on the basis of supply chain efficiency and vendor minimum implications. The results equaled a 21% reduction in sales and a 32% increase in costs to transport those remaining items to their destinations. The devil is in the detail, and if you are not careful, and knowledgeable of the cause and affect theory, you can leave a potential catastrophe in the wake of such well-intended decisions.

Your distribution center is an extension of your supply chain management controls. Take the necessary steps and appoint either a seasoned professional in the field of planning, allocation, merchandise and supply chain or institute a balanced committee to have equal jurisdiction in the evaluation and recommendation of the changes that are proposed. The committee would be best served with personnel who have first hand knowledge of the collective space they govern, and the openness to communicate issues and recommendations for amicable resolutions. If the power is slanted, the objectives are doomed to create a false hood towards the goals and expectations. But you need not worry if this happens to you, I or one of my esteemed colleagues will be there to steer the ship right once again.

By now you have probably realized that the title I assigned to this subject is a misnomer. The functionality of your conduit between your vendors and your stores, or final destination point, has very little to do with the labeling of such as a Distribution Center or Warehouse; and everything to do with synchronization of demand and flow. For years the practice of synchronizing the replenishment and allocation of merchandise through the warehouse to their destination has been seen as a separate function to the demand and flow cost composition. Although discussed by many executives as the largest exposure of dormant capital in the supply chain, the objective to increase fill rates trumps the quest for a scientific measurement of consumer demand satisfaction rate or CDSR. And thus the cycle of chase, fix and repeat becomes the status of many of these business units.

When you think about the incredible advancements that have been made in the field of technology as it relates to the consumer demand patterns and forecast accuracy, you have to understand the relational applications to your current processes and staffing. Too often I have been approached to fix the most mundane and rudimentary issues related to reducing inventory costs and improving turns without the involvement of the entire team. To alleviate issues and provide sustainable, quick wins, the problem's cure must come in concert with the issues that are causing the relative symptoms. Your distribution center's trailer bottlenecks are NOT caused by the inefficiencies to unload trailers fast enough. They are inherently caused by the lack of team involvement in the synchronization of the pipeline capacity forecast process. Timing, not quantity, becomes a realization 95% of the times that I have analyzed this common predicament.

When the focus is shifted from the operational capacity of your centers to the task of reducing store out of stocks, responding quicker and with purpose to store operation policy changes the answers provide a cure to the capacity question indirectly. The most common results are generally coupled to a streamlined flow process and order cycle refinement to ensure sustainability. The benefits from such an approach are substantial and measurable.

You not only alleviate the symptoms, you cure the cancerous affect of not fully engaging the science between the consumers wants and the ability to respond efficiently through your DC/Warehouse. When you try to separate the individual patterns of demand, at the store, warehouse and vendor, you derive a chart that is diametrically opposed and directly related to the very issue you wish to resolve. And yet, most retailers will admit that their focus is generally set to devise a way to match the ebbs and flow based on historical attributes and forecasted pattern isolations.

Think of it this way, if your warehouse replenishment system is an aggregate of demand patterns from the stores alone that it services, you've missed. Follow me on this, all right the items are ordered on time, received on time and put away in a timely manner. Now the question becomes when will the item be picked, packed and shipped to the stores and how quickly will the store have it located for the customer? When disparate processes are not properly synchronized and attuned to the specifics of your company's distribution and allocation processes, you will not reap the benefits of the time and investments into more technologically advanced systems and personnel.

The randomness of the individual stores is hidden in the global demand pattern applied to the individual sku or item being evaluated. This often-misunderstood process will eventually produce an aesthetically pleasing graph, but that is because the consumer demand patterns have equalized...meaning the customers have given up on that store and gone shopping elsewhere. So yes, you have diminished the span between demand and fulfillment but at what cost? When you posses a myopic focus to one issue, you lose sight of the only reason you are employed...your consumer.

Chapter 22

Leveraging Existing Systems

It is nothing more than human nature; alive and well in the corporation's of America.   When something isn't working the way we expect, or want it to; our first inclination is to replace the defective relic with something *shiny* and new.   Let's face it, in our non-business lives if one diet doesn't work we'll try another, and another, and well, you get my point.   The same holds true in business, and why should it be any different?   Because hundreds and often times thousands of individual associates rely on good sound business judgments by appointed executives to preserve market share and reduce costs.   And yet there is irrefutable evidence throughout recent history in retail showing that the first line of action is to replace a system, process and/or technology at the very hint of something gone wrong.   Recognizing the true causal issues, and not just dealing with the loudest symptoms will greatly reduce capital expenditures, workloads and cash flow disruptions.

I have been hard pressed to find a retailer out there that hasn't improved their information gathering processes via updated POS registers and larger more powerful data collecting servers and systems over the past five years. But for all of those efforts, many companies have leveraged the banking covenants by investing in the next great technology presented by a well meaning, but single focused, software vendor. Providing visibility to your issues without the adaptation of control factors to guide the decision process only allows you to see the cliff well in advance getting your brakes fixed. You will be braced in advance, but your going over...

I have witnessed some of the greatest forms of what I call *Frankenstein* technology compositions that I believe have ever been created by mankind. These are what are often referred to as *bolt-on* modules professing to alleviate everything from stock-outs to price optimization, to markdown improvements. Don't get me wrong; I am a huge advocate of the *Best of Breed* approach to system improvements, but you have to know *when* to say *when*. Just because the users feel good about the sales pitch they were given, doesn't mean that you can't take a second look under the hood. If you're not comfortable with identifying what's there, hire a professional just to review your team's findings. You want to the best possible understanding of what your company is getting and how it works with the strategic objectives. In a nutshell it has to focus on improving information collaboration and what I call the **One house, One rule** process to ensuring equilibrium obtainment between business units.

Inventory issues will always find their way back to their source. Even if you are able to apply technology to some of the symptoms, the core issue will soon resurrect its ugly head. To ensure the proper path is followed by your users as to where they are taking the company, you must exercise due diligence to understand from which you came and where you need to be. If the new allocation system is causing too much inventory to accumulate in the wrong stores, the symptom may show up as a service level issue. Thus, a false positive could surface that an improved system is needed to mitigate the out of stocks in the distribution center.

No, the issue is within your processes and/or technology governing the method of distribution to the stores. Without a guru of inventory and systems on staff, you may not recognize the underlying issues and falsely elect to quiet the symptom. For an honest, low cost evaluation, employ several consultants under the guideline of obtaining practical solution information. Have them evaluate the end-to-end current process for no more than (2) two weeks and provide their recommendations. Then align their resolutions with a third independent consultant for a final evaluation. I know this sounds like a lot, but trust me that a more impartial, well thought out and documented resolution cannot be accomplished within most corporations and certainly not as quickly with relatively little down time to your team's daily objectives.

The goal will be to assemble the information from an unbiased representative to ensure that the causal effect of your described issue isn't being hidden due to personal or professional ideology within the company. Again, you are working with human beings, and self-preservation isn't always a completely conscious effort. So you may hear what they want you to hear. To bring the best possible answer out of many good / great ideas, you sometimes need a *judge* who has heard the *plaintiffs* before, but has the wisdom to acknowledge the customer's needs and rationalize your team's ability to satisfy them.

Often it is found by a lot of chief information officers when confronted with yet another business requirement from the team is that the information is willing, but the applications are not able. Basically this means that the data is already there to answer the questions of the day, however the systems are not configured to deliver the information to the user community. In these cases, more often than not, the answer comes in the form of an incomplete; irrational acceptance of a sales pitch that appeals to the emotional side of the user community. The resulting operations rarely equal the initial portrayal due to the fact that the tactical and technical side had nothing to do with the lights, smoke and mirrors that were portrayed.

Make sure that you are getting the most out of your existing systems by ensuring that your personnel are well versed and trained on the applications. Many companies have similar systems in their technology graveyards because the new régime had a comfort zone using a particular application. Do not allow the lack of knowledge dictate your expense and time of implementing a duplicate system. Know your stuff, or hire someone who can provide an expert opinion on what you have and offer ways to get more out of what you already have.

Systems, by nature, are devised with similar aspects to their functionality and premise. When you break down the components of any system offering, you will find that the core values rely on the only (3) things that matter; or should matter to your business. **Recognize** the key consumer demand patterns and their relationship to your supply chain. **Optimize** the value proposition of the customer relationships you wish to foster within your niche. **Effectively** and efficiently manage an ongoing process enhancement campaign to educate and motivate your teams on cash management.

Continuous and monitored improvements to your existing processes will enable you to better recognize the need for improvements or replacement of your current systems. Without fully understanding where it is you company wants or needs to go, you can't possibly quantify the implementation of another rogue system. Use what you have until the use of such constitutes a willful and malice act of mediocrity. In other words, finding a better way to harness your mule to pull the plow isn't at all what we are discussing here.

Move the team into a higher level of science and technology by all means. But if the new technology is a re-make of the former benchmark process, and you will know this by asking the seller from which system their technology is patterned from, get that system and educate your users. An educated user group will always...always trump a system full of technical prowess. Look at it this way, if the system could do everything that is claimed in the sales pitch...why aren't they using it in a retail environment themselves and making the millions they claim to be able to save you?

Chapter 23

Open To Buy
Wrong Business Model For Today's Retail

A h yes, the proverbial forecast and reporting holy grail of merchandise division operations from far and wide. This instrument has often been deemed the weekly checks and balances guideline. Where you often get a thumbs up or down on a Monday morning based on last week's business that sets the tone for the rest of the week. This process is the last bastion of comfort for the weary buyer and divisional leader who are not sure as to the financial stature of their entrusted domain. For those of you who are not familiar with this topic, the Open To Buy is a functional monitor, somewhat of a *checkbook* register.

An open forum or window of the business activities of inflow and outflow of cash based on a financial amount bestowed upon them from the CFO and Executive leadership. The intent of this monitor is to help align your business practices with the needs and responsibilities assigned to your business unit. In actuality it is a harbinger of bad habits and impulse reactionary mistakes that have plagued the merchandise divisions for years.

Allow me to explain. Those who are in the business are all aware that the process of planning is initiated with the analysis and construction of a sales plan. This sales plan consists of many assumptions and objectives based on top down and bottom up statistics. The utilization of historical facts control much of the directional flow of your weekly and monthly sales targets while the turn and gmroi, gross margin return on inventory investments, guide your inventory flow, initial pricing, markdowns and final liquidation. Now you may hear many different versions and a litany of drawn out pontifications to the above illustration. But when it is all said and done, the dollars given to invest in inventory should and must garnish a higher return than the expenses to procure, deliver and sell the merchandise. All of which, is captured in my illustration of the process above.

Here is where I depict the fallacy. The majority of open to buy processes, and thus software to enable such practices are built on an unconventional time and action chart called a twelve month or (52/53) week annual basis depending on a leap year. I am not here to cast blame on those who initiated this process, like many processes before this, there was a time and place when the practicality and usefulness of it made all the sense in the world. Those times are now gone.

Because of this practice, the flow of merchandise was almost predestined to come in heavy at the first of the month and taper off towards the end of the month. The culprit? *Inventory Turn*... You see the erroneous emphasis on monthly turn objectives in the open to buy provided a falsehood to those who were forced to obey. The implication was that the sooner you brought the goods in during a particular month, the more time you had to sell through the inventory and thus improve the turn of your merchandise. In some of the low average dollar, high unit movement corporations; the emphasis is on the consumer's who have a pattern to shop the first of the month and thus promotional cadence is aligned. This however has a more positive affect in the dollar store channel due to the magnitude of the lift experienced during the first of each month. Their business is disproportionately aligned with federal checks and the harmonized monthly budgeting of their customers. The term lift is a quantifiable ratio portrayed as an index to a normalized period of comparison. For instance, a 1.45 lift to last week would indicate that the performance was 45% better than the comparison week.

Now lets discuss the alternative and more accurate way to evaluate your inventory productivity. If you are using an open to buy, you're half way there already. The changes will be seamless to most users and will accomplish your goals with a longer span of time and faster, more consumer centric demand pattern responses. There is no need to initially run out and invest in the newest shiny technology with the efforts barely equaling the results. If your process is not optimized, the speed at which you make mistakes may be enhanced by a new technology, however the accuracy will be only slightly improved.

Today's retail is much more volatile than just a few years ago with a few months dictating your trajectory rather than the historic cycle of this year versus last year. The first enhancement you need to implement against your monthly open to buy is a weekly forecast. This rather simple, yet dynamic interface will serve several important functions. First, it will illuminate the impact of inventory purchasing plans with far more cost conscious visibility than a monthly target. Your *front-loading* inventory receipt efforts will show boldly and brightly and allow for conversations to take place on smoothing efforts. You will be able to follow the purchase orders or planned receipts all the way from assortment rationalization, through the cash flow impact of initial display quantities and relevant sales expectations. Second, your team will be better educated on the individual decision making processes and their impact to the corporation's cash reserves.

The control mechanism is the G.M.R.O.I. or Gross Margin Return On Investment. When evaluated on a weekly basis, the productivity of inventory during a sale promotion, markdown strategy or new receipt can be quickly optimized. You can't predict the monthly demand of an item or category accurately on a consistent basis. Therefore the rules of engagement have to be applied to the reaction and speed by which your team converges on reactionary business rules following the weekly signals.

Best Practice

The statistics gathered by this supplemental module can then be linked to your current open to buy process. The forecast engine, I have found, is best when it is constructed to utilize the dynamics of a (78) week index controlled rolling process. The initial (26) weeks of your module are lagging or most current past weeks. In some venues we call those actual weeks. These weeks have a comparison to the adjacent weeks from last year. When I say adjacent, I am referring to the corresponding holiday, promotion, natural disaster or other known event for that weekly period. The most accurate calculation I have found is the use of historical dynamic linear regression with standard deviation used as a pivot point.

Your model will have (78) weeks of rolling historical net sales, in units and dollars, from this you will derive the average selling retail against inventory. You will have a plan for net sales, inventory, receipts, markdowns and gross margin dollars derived from your monthly open to buy initially. The key variable for a successful weekly forecast is the placement and use of an Impact Index that controls each week's calculated forecast. This index is simple in nature, but extremely beneficial when future changes are known. Such as, new store openings, closings, new promotions, product category changes, advertising adjustments..etc.

The use of the index will allow you to target a week, or a series of weeks to perform a little stronger or weaker than the current trend of performance. The beauty of this is that the aggregate can be from the top down, in the illustration of stores opening or closing, or at a specific category when promotions or fresh new product is introduced or you are about to anniversary such an event and need a reduction.

The operation should not be so complex that you need a team of scientist to understand and interpret the majority of the users, yet be stringent enough to allow for the practice of bottom up, top down and middle out weekly impacts. The accuracy of the weekly forecasts will be logged and noted against future estimates; the better the improved forecasts, the less deviation to the numbers that are calculated. This removes the emotional, or hypothetical process of today's monthly forecasts and allows the consumer and the corporation's objectives dictate the flow on inventory and the impacts on the entire supply chain.

Make no mistake about it; this is one tool that no corporation should be without when attempting to control their financial destiny. However, it is just a tool. To reap the benefits and rewards from such a tool you will need to recognize, hire and retain the best and brightest trainer, partner and leader; and then progressively get out of their way.

Chapter 24

Opportunities

Riddled with Risks, Rewards and Complexities

There was a time, not so long ago, that when you heard someone utter the phrase; "We have an *opportunity...*" it inferred that there was something very positive to be gained by taking advantage of the situation. In today's environment, as we have been bamboozled and hoodwinked into accepting things for face value, and paying the ultimate price of our time and money for such insolents, we now question everything. Sometimes to our own detriment; for as it has been said in business and life's lessons continuously remind us, you are either quick and adjust accordingly; or you're playing catch-up or perish.

So, how do we risk the chance for obtainable rewards when the guarantee for such only exists on paper or word-of-mouth? Can we reduce the complexities of in-depth, costly and long drawn out analysis that typically result in a point; counter point debate? How is it that your competitors appear to continuously evolve their systems, processes and personnel semi-annually and you are still struggling with 19th century technology and thus ideas? The answer is very simple when you apply the questions to the humanistic side of your business and remove the cloak of corporate business units and divisions.

In our pursuit to formalize and structure our corporate entities, we often hinder ourselves when we instill policies, procedures and guidelines. No! I am not going to suggest that you shouldn't have theses structures, but what I will tell you is that we often get what we wish for. You see when we have a plan, or a project that has been reviewed, accepted and adopted; we find it difficult to veer away from our plan. More to the point, in business and more pointedly the business of retail we demand that the plan is particularly adhered to with the threat of severe punishment and even dismissal.

Well now, what do you think an opportunity is to one's plan? Hmmmm? That's right, it constitutes a deviation and thus is naturally suppressed by many and discarded by most even if there is a potential positive out come. That is also why there is generally such rigorous opposition to opportunities today from many sides of the aisle. You can't steel home if you're told to stop at first base, even though from your perspective the opposing team's outfielder is having trouble locating the ball!

Think about your own everyday financial activities. When you began investing, hopefully dollar cost averaging was your chosen method of adding to your portfolio balance. In short, that means having the same amount of dollars invested on a consistent monthly basis in an effort to accumulate shares without trying to pick the highs and lows of the market. Your 401k or other similar investment vehicle utilizes this common practice. Now take a look at the opportunity to INCREASE your dollar amount when the market is low. Did you do that? Most investors have not taken advantage of these opportunities, which have been so abundant lately.

The market drops 200 points one day and many investors stop their automatic investments for fear that it will go lower…then begin investing again when it recovers. Why? Because the adopted plan called for moderate volatility and when the gyrations became too intense, we mitigate our risk of deviation from the plan. See the fallacy here? The opportunity is to buy low and sell high, everyone knows this, but only a few reap the rewards by looking into the future and contemplate the likelihood of the market staying down for an extended period of time. Armed with such knowledge, the opportunity is to increase contributions when it's down below a threshold, call it 11,000 and go back to normal contributions when it hits 12,500.

The same holds true in businesses when the opportunity calls for a deviation to the plan. Unless a concrete position can be made for the change, it is met with obstacles that will stifle creativity and promote the status quo. Comparing the risks to the rewards is a task best left to the unemotional and strategic minded. There are generally (3) three questions to be asked when confronted with an opportunity.

1. Does this opportunity provide an R.O.I. in (90) days or less?
2. Can it be executed from order to first sale in (30) days or less?
3. Is the exit strategy costs on par with our minimum margin requirements?

After those 3 key questions, the rest become more social and aesthetic in nature like, does this fit our mantra? or can we place the merchandise around the check-outs? Which are meaningful and important question, but the bottom line is; WILL WE MAKE MONEY in a timely manner?

I hope that you paid particularly close attention to the third question on my list. This is by far one of the most common reasons for a failed strategy, and why myopic leaders become wary to step outside of the box. This may sound cliché but everything *doesn't* always go as planned. Therefore, you have to have contingency plans already in the pipeline. You are not planning for failure, and please put this on the table immediately. On the contrary, you are simply ensuring the solvency of the project if and when key objectives of the process are not met. It may not be an indication of a bad idea as much as it may be the wrong time. Be sure to maintain high energy levels during this phase of the discussions. Energy is fed upon and become infectious when accompanied by the right attitude towards providing support. Try not to get too caught up in the resolution planning and provide *what-if* scenarios as if you already have the answers.

By providing clear and concise expectations, the complexities of growing and/or changing the business become more of an academic exercise and reduce the emotional suggestions substantially. Just be sure to leave your ego at the door. Your team can and will produce, it may not be EXACTLY how you would do it, or maybe it will take a little longer to achieve the intended results, but if you exercise patients and perseverance, the future rewards from the team gaining confidence and resolving issues on their own will have triple the payback.

To be a successful leader that overcomes obstacles and accepts opportunities, you have to focus on the job of producing the right initiatives, and then having those strategies carried out by your associates. Although many leaders today strive to have all the right answers, it is not necessary. The goal is to ask the right questions and establish a line of communication that embraces the different views and ideas amongst the team. By nurturing and providing encouragement when necessary, your team will follow your lead as a role model. The key differentiator is the ability to listen and respond with empathy.

Your process of establishing and building upon your relationships is hinged on your responses to your people and the problems. The moment most leaders get into trouble is when they lower the bar due to low expectations in an attempt to build morale. The associates are always watching your moves to gain insight on the person, but what is more important, they want to follow someone who has a proven ability to change when needed, and remain true to the principles of character they have come to be known for.

Presenting and judging opportunities is sometimes far more complicated than simply gauging the effective return on investment. With all the potential risks, rewards and complexities, you have to provide the proper instructions and motivational qualities that will sustain the decisions, even when they don't work out as anticipated. Creating an indelible roadmap for your team to follow is critical to the longevity and productivity of your objectives and responsibilities as the leader of the business.

I was very fortunate to have learned early in my career from a fantastic array of mentors. They taught me that when you take on a position of responsibility, you perform up to and beyond the scope of the position; without hesitation.   From them I learned the value of embracing new ideas and judging the outcome of decisions by a different standard. I do so based on the course correction taken when issues arise, and do not criticize the team for the fact that there *was* an issue. In order for the team to grow and continue to reach for opportunities, they must keep leaning. The will to learn manifests from the freedom to make mistakes and recover from them without judgmental interludes along the way.

No one will ever remember the resolved issues; they will only remember the outcome of the venture. Once you have established the proper core principles for the organization to follow, you need not track their every move. That autonomy will transcend most of the issues that they will face. Their confidence will guide them and the future success of the team is all but certain. There will always be unforeseen pressures on the team to produce. What is expected from everyone on the team, including you, is that the decisions will always be guided by standards. These standards include the ethical behavior you have made clear through your words and your actions. This will become the prevailing winds against the sails towards mitigating the **risks**, obtaining the **rewards** and reducing the **complexities** affiliated with **opportunities**.

Chapter 25

Do People Really Matter?

During the formidable economic turmoil years of 2008 through 2013, many human resource managers will face the challenge of retaining and motivating their corporation's best people. They will be required to do so in the midst of layoffs, nearly nonexistent wage increases and business unit downsizing. For them, this will be the Achilles heal to maintaining a healthy corporate morale and a major leadership challenge of the next cyclical economic boom periods of 2014 - 2020. The latter part of 2008 through the end of 2012 will see bedrock corporations crumble and loyal 20+ year associates dislodged into an unemployment and economic downturn not before witnessed; and soon forgotten era.

However, the initial damage done to the *loyalty* factor will play heaviest on our young associates. They will no longer share a loyalty towards their corporation as they witnessed the outcome of such loyalty time and time again. The evidence of the trend has been shown and will only increase in the employee turnover statistics and job dissatisfaction aggregate percentages in 2012 & 2013. As the economic recovery begins to formulate, businesses will be forced to do more on the job training and offer incentives to attract and retain a shrunken workforce. The workers will be attracted to the highest bidder for what is important to the associate; money, time and/or perks. Tenure at an organization that cannot increase morale will be measured in months, not years as the shuffle to greener pastures ensues.

It's not all gloom and doom; the positive value here is that happy, satisfied associates do not equal good morale. Morale is a derivative of the group's ability to engage their emotions in a positive manner to accomplish their goals and expectations as assigned. For instance, firefighters can exhibit a high morale during the process of evacuating a burning building using their training and communication skills. Very few of them enter a life-threatening situation with a smile of happiness and contentment on their faces, and yet their morale can be measurably higher than most associates in an organization. With that in mind, leaders will be most effective during this recovery if they focus their efforts on providing clear, concise directions to the teams and manage expectations within the realm of available resources and time.

Communication will once again be a key differentiator of those who are true leaders going forward versus those who are simply appointed to lead. The sign of a great communicator is having and/or taking the necessary time to illustrate the actions of the organization consistently and with open, honest Q&A during such interactions. It is easy to collect the team for a positive announcement; but can you gather the same workforce and announce layoffs due to a forecasted economic lackluster period ahead? Condition yourself to deal with the facts, not the emotions. Illustrate the term of the impact either with head count, date and/or objective so that finality is understood and expectations are established.

Your communications will be most effective when you are able to pull adjoined business units into the same conversations. Each area will be better poised to aligning efficiencies when they understand how the baton is passed and the impacts of failed objectives not only to their team, but the teams that react in sequence to the other business units.

Encourage individual area problem solving and issue resolution. No one person has all of the insight and answers for the best possible decision to a business unit's issue. Unless they are intricately involved and perform the very task being reviewed day in and day out, their perspective can be helpful, but should remain as a suggestive foundation and not a resolution. Again, communicate this amongst the teams; not just the initiating group. You will find that this may answer a common theme of issues in other areas, or at the very least find that the resolution causes another team to revamp their role in the hand-off phase.

The smartest associates are not always the most vocal. The more that you can enforce the policy of *no bad ideas* the more interaction you will receive from the best and the brightest! Above all else, keep the teams motivated in understanding that the tough times will only make you stronger on the other side, and that today's most impossible issues will become yesterday's news in 24 hours...*and then comes tomorrow*.

Staffing for a new era!

Among the most influential human resource associates I have had the pleasure of working with was someone who absolutely understood people. She knew that the corporate culture didn't just happen because of some mantra that existed; it had to be nurtured and recited constantly. Combine this challenge with a CEO that was driven by statistics and the ability to achieve more with less, and you have an almost perfect storm against positive morale. Your prospects of running a successful and dynamic organization diminish rapidly when the associates recognize that the company lacks a commitment to genuinely treat them with the dignity and respect afforded them as human beings first.   Many leaders lose the functional concept of such actions because they substitute the need to understand the individual values and beliefs of the team with the strategy and objectives of the business unit.   The associates in turn, perform at an acceptable level and provide very little in terms of their hearts and souls in accomplishing a goal.   This tepid attempt to perform is generally evident in the financial performances produced by these teams.

What I believe to be a foundational core to our societal and thus job related acceptance of complacency, is the misguided impact of the entitlement thought processes. Somewhere in the last (10 – 15) years we have completely transitioned from;

"Win one for the Gipper", which was a sort of team battle cry from coach Knute Rockne during a football half time speech at Notre Dame University 1928, to *"What have you done for* **ME** *lately?"*...Janet Jackson, Jimmy Jam and Terry Lewis collaboration 1986 - Control...

Unless the associates feel that there is some immediately tangible benefit to him/her for doing something above and beyond their minimum job requirements, they will manage to keep themselves and the team on a course for mediocrity.   To segregate your company from those that foster such behavior, you have to MAKE time to get to know your associates. You no longer can rely on the past to understand the current and future workforce social, family and economic conditions.

Previous to the past (10 – 15) years, you could assume that a large portion of your workforce had traditional values, aspirations and functioned under the same creeds as their peers and leadership. You could offer a benefit like {time and a half} for (4) hours of overtime tonight and feel that you had everyone's acceptance. Today's associates have children in after school care or other support functions so that they as single parent workers or dual income families can survive. So with that in mind you can now see why the seemingly generous time and a half offered won't cover half of the additional costs that will be incurred to due late, or last minute arrangements needed to secure their family's well being.

As much as business leaders would like to have a clear separation of work and home, there will always be a need to recognize, understand and cultivate the two in the most effective and efficient manner. There will always be a time when additional workforce efforts are needed, and it is at those times that a discussion needs to occur to rationalize the best possible way to achieve this. It may be an earlier start, later day, weekend or two or three…whatever it takes. You will have much more acceptance and productivity if the team helps to formulate the resolution. Put the issue on the table, the cause, and the facts surrounding the situation and open the floor for discussions. You will find that this journey will be very meaningful in cultivating the teams cultures, beliefs and strengthen the team's resolve to understanding the all important; WHY.

You may be one of those fortunate few who have the voice and the ability to capture attention and retain interest when you speak. But that is a rare quality that is bestowed upon few, and recognized and utilized by even fewer. To educate and train your team, you will have to be balanced with your timing and the environment you've chosen to deliver your address. To ensure your intended results occur, you must be aware of, and remain sensitive to the place and manner in which you engage the teams. A common practice is to put yourself in their shoes and pay particularly close attention to the way you use certain words and the context by which they are chosen.

Never be afraid to illustrate the truth and utilize the facts, as they are known at the time. Leaving things up for interpretations is a very dangerous and reckless practice and should be avoided at all times. If you notice that there is a lot of head turning, frowning and rolling of eyes by the teams during your delivery; stop and question those who are guilty of such actions why they feel that there is something wrong in what you have said thus far. Perhaps they heard a different story around the water cooler, or someone heard what they THOUGHT to be a truth around a corner from the chief's office. Either way, address it and allow all to reach the same conclusions based on a single version of the truth.

Unlike wine, bad news tends not to improve with age. In fact it quickly becomes rancid and can become almost too strong to replace if left to fester for too long. For this reason I would highly recommend that you dictate your information as quickly as possible. The rumor mill can produce 100 pounds of falsehoods before you can deliver an ounce of truth. Don't try to creatively detour something that has run-a-muck in your organization. Address it head on, no matter how ugly the truth of the issue may be.

Remember, personal matters are only personal until they cause morale issues; then they become business matters and must be addressed accordingly. That's a far cry from the 90's as we developed out of the also poor economic conditions of the mid to late 80's. But as I have stated before and will continue to illuminate, change is the one constant in our lives that has purpose if you understand it properly and is inevitable.

When you and your team are capable of embracing change for what it truly is; the incubator for success, you will begin the process of mastering your future. Change is a lot like a raging river, approach it without recognizing its power and you will succumb to its might negative forces. Embrace it and harness the abundance of strength and power and you can use it to your benefit to produce electricity and provide recreation.

The rules of engagement when dealing with our people have changed exponentially. That which we once held as sacred cows are now historical markers of a time when. This magnitude of change in a relatively short amount of time is not an easy transition, and some may never make the leap.

To ensure that your team is ready, willing and able to learn, it is crucial that you have chosen the members carefully. Find strengths and weaknesses that will compliment the growth of the team. Motivate the quiet and structure their focus on tomorrow. Yesterday belongs to history, the future has yet to be written and the control is theirs to command. The team will persevere with patience and resolve towards consistent efforts. Provide a roadmap of such that can assist the team in understanding where they came from, where they are now and where we need them to be.

Make your milestones frequent in the beginning and extend them as the project matures. As they begin to taste the victory of the short hits, they will grow hungrier as the time elongates between accomplishments. Know your teams well; do not dangle the carrot for too long. Know their limitations and how well they can gather their senses and begin marching once again. Too little intervention and the team will bore into mediocrity. Too much and they will resolve from the pressures to mediocrity.

Know your business and know your people....

Because they really do matter!

Chapter 26

Factors For Business Survival

For more years than I care to recall, companies have made the fundamental mistake of allowing the organizational charts dictate their protocol for strategies. For instance, the most senior personnel of a business unit called Merchandising are awarded the task of making all product decisions and pricing strategies for the corporation. Now, I am not taking anything away from the acumen or talent bestowed on the vast majority of the personnel affiliated with the merchandising department. But the fact of the matter is, they are typically psychological and emotional beings by nature. They're just not exactly built for the arduous task of strategic process thinking, with bottom line impacts, cost of capital constraints and return on equity evaluations.

Without the proper structure, their decisions are not always statistically based and tend to follow a traditional and emotional process. This is rarely best for the corporation and often results in the difference between good and GREAT corporations. When the structure not only allows for, but also is dependent upon a process of procedures that gathers relevant data from the price optimization area, surveys the store or sales personnel and market basket data and at some point copulates this with the executive guidance and observations for strategic future growth, success is much more likely.

Remember that just because the senior vice president of merchandising and the senior vice president of store operations may switch positions and roles in the organization, doesn't autonomously grant your company successful decision making.   The vision of placing strengths into opposing business units has a shred of occupational brilliance, and a host of strategic and team building issues. Without the organizational structure to support the lack of expertise each person would bring to their new realm of the business, the knowledge constraints and learning curves will hinder the overall progress of the organization.   Several billion dollar plus retail organizations have attempted this very strategy, not surprisingly they all failed miserably. The key factors that were overlooked when transitioning the organization for such a different focus was the lack of meaningful communication, controlling expectations and mitigating initial judgments.

To successfully transition the company into the new structure, which by the way has tremendous merits, you would first apply what's called collaborative team acceptance measures. Simply put, the associates who will be directed by the new SVP would be given a voice in how, when and where the transition would be performed. This would allow the groups to take ownership of the process on behalf of the corporation's success and remove the plight of feeling like;

"here comes another bad idea whose time will come to fail if we ignore it and wait long enough".

"This was an actual quote from an associate involved in such a transitional corporate switch."

Failure can simply happen during change due to unforeseen circumstances beyond your control, or those who resent or neglect to understand the value of the change can induce it. The key factors for business survival here are to first, know that your idea for change is based on the evaluation of immediate knowledge versus the advent of future knowledge.

Never place the trajectory of your company on the aspects of leaders who have yet to grow the fundamental relationships of their domain. You don't want to give authority too soon to a newly appointed leader in the company or business unit. And second, always make available the arena and latitude for the organization to know and ask questions as to what's happening, when it is to happen and ultimately why it is right for the company.

As you carefully transition the organization into the current vision, you will want to be on the lookout for your next level of management successors. It is during these opportunistic times that true leadership will be revealed to you through the decision making processes and the team's migration towards the one or two associates that warrant their attention. Provide just enough intervention to keep the processes flowing, but resist the urge to bring them too far too fast. It is during the trials of dealing with unexpected and uncomfortable decisions that the unbiased and visionary leaders are created.

Here is something that you may wish to apply when given the opportunity. During one of my endeavors to educate my team, I utilized the process of role-playing. The twist I put on it was to have a few members role-play as executive members of our most highly regarded competitors. The results from giving them a motivation that they, being the role-players in this exercise, were having double digit comp store increases versus our corporation's negative and low single digit comp store increases, what are they saying about our corporation in their meetings? I no sooner sad "go" when immediately one of the associates ran with my idea and took it beyond my expectations by scrunching up his face and saying;

"..didn't I tell you (*x-company*),{which was our organization}, would fall behind us in sales this month again?" *laughter..*

By this time it was pretty obvious to me what executive from our number one competitor he was attempting to impersonate, but I couldn't wait to hear more. And to my delight, he continued.

"They insist on trying to sell the same merchandise over and over to a customer base that is stagnant." "How many widgets can a family own...even if you put them on sale for 50% off, they will only purchase one and enjoy the saving. You can't grow the top, or bottom lines that way!!" *laughter..*

Behold, your associates know what is causing your corporation's mediocre sales and stagnant margin issues. They are being spoken to honestly by their family, friends and neighbors who shop your stores daily. Your executives are not receiving the same honest banter from their relationships in the community because of their status in some instances, and because their neighbors do not shop at the stores related to your executives.

Provide your associates with a venue to open up and illustrate their information and concerns in a manner that does not persecute them. Begin by making it anonymous at first, and then as trust begins to build, attach a value to the divulgence of usable information. Keep it simple, half a day off with pay, $100 cash, or maybe a free voucher for lunch for 4 at a local restaurant. You'll be amazed at what issues lurk just beneath your line of visibility and awareness.

Much of what you need to know is just a conversation away, but you must possess the skills and ability to extract that conversation from the right person at the right time. Taking an associate to lunch to gather information is rarely a tactic that works for most employers. Although it is the most popular methodology in practice today, the same and even more compelling information can be extracted through a series of chats while eating a snack, drinking a soda or just walking around the warehouse or office with this person to gain insight.

Understand that your vision, and that of the company can only come to fruition when your people are focused and passionate about what their role is and why they are important to its' completion. Resist the urge to adopt a strategy of managing issues through the use of a committee. I hope that if we learned anything from the Obama presidency term it is that the ultimate decision maker must finally have the closing word and is the owner of the strategy going forward. We witnessed so many hang-ups and failed attempts to correct our plight due to politics and indecisions during the 2008 – 2012 term; the majority of the country became dissatisfied and resented the whole notion of politics. The same resentment and mediocrity will unveil itself within the four walls of your organization if there is not a clear, concise and consistent example of leadership decision-making.

Unfortunately, spreading responsibility so that you have equal power amongst your divisions tends to equate to equal blame and stagnant growth over time.
    –U.S. Congress 2008 – 2012-

Do your best not to confuse the words *strategic* and *visionary* as you explain your goals to the group. Although these two words are commonly used interchangeably amongst business leaders, they have separate meanings. When you are illustrating your corporation's vision, you are depicting a particular position for the organization to be obtained and maintained. You then follow that expression with a series of passionate communications that will reinforce your vision.

The plan or roadmap that will be utilized to obtain your vision is called your strategy. To ensure success of your strategy, all stakeholders must be educated on their role towards completion and how important their individualism is to accomplishing the vision. I fully believe that when you have the full support of your people, and they understand your vision and are laser focused on the strategies aligned to ensure success, it's hard to miss an objective. Because of the aforementioned, your teams will be ready to shift when necessary and hold the helm through rough seas. Even if your strategy isn't quite right, the organization will enjoy the success of the journey and learn many more valuable lessons from the mistakes than if the strategy was perfect and the team was disjointed. Focus on communicating your vision, and then communicate your strategy! ...*Repeat*...

Mistakes are healthy

How's your appetite for risk? Have you asked yourself whether you would rather be first inline for something, or are you more of the mindset of you'll get there when you get there and allow fate to control your destiny? If you equate yourself closest to the latter than to the former, you may not need to be in a leadership role of a retail establishment or business.

If your group isn't taking risks, your not getting the most out of the team. Yes you're correct; risks insure that mistakes will be made. It is a packaged deal. However, your role and indeed responsibility to the organization as a leader is to encourage the proper level of risk taking amongst your teams. Many leaders measure the individual impacts of each mistake made and not the global impact of the success rate versus failures. A well-placed calculated risk in the marketing area can add tremendously to the revenue stream of the organization. These risks are lost to a lot of corporations due to the improper evaluation of the outcome of failed risk ventures of the past.

You must evaluate the mishap based on what was known, to whom and when to give a proper evaluation of the issue. Without a full case revue of the decision process, you are creating a void that will surely swallow all of the maverick ideas and compelling benefits from your teams. The adage, learn from your mistakes, assumes that you have knowledge of what went wrong. Without the benefit of stewardship in breaking down the situation, identifying the issues and illustrating the corrective course for success, you may not want to take too many risks. But of course, that's the wrong position because it is the birthplace of mediocrity. Position your leadership and strategies to be able to take risks.

Don't just announce that you want more risk taking out there. Encourage your teams to make timelier decisions on their own with the knowledge that they follow the corporation's vision, gather *enough* prevailing data, and make corrections when necessary. The alternative is for a morale stifling process that requires a litany of approvals that assumes the final decision will be perfect and that they won't be too late to take advantage of the window of opportunity.

Because I was fortunate to have been mentored by some of the most capable, caring and intellectually advanced leaders during my career, I feel obligated to share. Mr. John Reier, one of the greatest retail executives and merchants of our times, and my mentor once said to me that;

"Attitude is the difference between great leaders and the positions they hold."

He made this comment to me very early on in my career and it held true all throughout my rank escalation. Your associates will get the job done if they respect the position, they will flourish when they respect the leader.

I learned more from the failures that I witnessed more so than I did from the successes. Although the successes were much more abundant, they began to become part of a more global equation as I pursued the opportunities for growth and development of my teams. The failures became part of the battles as I pursued the boundaries of that which most felt could not be accomplished with the resources available. I had the capacity, drive and determination to educate, train and ensure that our teams were second to none; with the right ATTITUDE.

I knew that from repetition would come expertise and from capacity improvements would come performance enhancement. But for all that I surveyed, analyzed and hypothesized; I am ever so grateful that luck was on my side. When you are finished with the high fives and pats on the back, remember that without the alignment of many uncontrollable factors, each decision point could follow many different directions.

By the grace of knowledge, influence and significant process evaluations your results are just a circumstance away from being an issue. But what will separate you in business will also separate you in life. It is how you deal with the issue and what is more important, what you do with that knowledge that is obtained during this all-important cycle.

Many times the circumstances that have proven to be career making for me, materialized because I had the audacity to not succumb to the neigh-sayers. Instead I would forge ahead based on analysis and understanding of the facts as I saw them. All the while prepared to admit my mistake, but what is more important, prepared with a resolution to the mistake. Uncertainty was, and will continue to consistently be the force that brought down most leaders and their people.

When you attempt to apply logic to an illogical condition you will find yourself exerting too much valuable time and resources. Such are the conditions of economics and emotions of the current day. Some of the leaders of great institutions have fallen from grace due to ambiguity and slow reaction to the matters at hand. To be an effective and responsible leader you must first recognize that the facts are essential, and the quantity of such are not as important as the quality. Too many facts can result in a dysfunctional effort when personnel from different fields of the organization or business unit portray their individualized versions of the truth.

Having the ability to recognize that the facts are real for each individual business unit as they see them, and being able to bring about a common mindset based on impact analysis is an art. The ideal preparation for being capable of disseminating the proper direction comes from experience in multiple facets of the business. Success comes from acquired and retained knowledge and is sustained through observations and education. Never stop learning from your environment and associates. Leadership is earned, you will find that most associates *respect* the *position*, but will f*ollow* a *leader* regardless of position or title.

Great Expectations of Leaders

Although there are many examples of great leaders in our history, each of them was created over time. None of them were *born leaders* as you have so often heard as an animated description of some managers. In order for an individual to meet and beat the expectations to become a great leader, they must first know how to identify and correct their weaknesses. If you do not feel that you have any weaknesses, that's where you will begin. If you have trouble identifying your own weaknesses, then ask your team to perform a pseudo 360 evaluation and in a single sentence, describe what you do that's wrong.

The great leaders focus on removing the complexities of the day-to-day business as presented through their associates. If you can quickly move towards increasing shareholder value through operational efficiencies, you will quickly compound those results. Confidence is restored through a means of adaptive communication focus efforts. As you recognize, openly acknowledge and reward the captains of each of the business units, you will see that the organization's strengths evolve around their practices and understanding of the process.

The skills and experience levels of each area have to be evaluated for effectiveness, elevated to the minimum standards of acceptance and then constantly challenged to grow. Enforce a practice of clarity of communication. To communicate does not simply mean that one person or group is talking and another is listening. Clarity of communication represents a faction that the parties are listening to what the other is saying and prepared to repeat what they heard when asked. This could be defined as the reading of the minutes after a meeting. It ensures that the words used, the way they were used and the assumptions formulated by the listeners were all on point.

Basically this puts forth a roadmap of actions and reactions that will help guide the team's efforts and progress. To simply issue a citation and leave it out there for interpretation is not communicating and is certainly not the action of a great leader.

You must leave *footprints* for your teams to follow if you want to achieve the expected results.

Just as we began our journey, so shall it end with the conclusion that no matter how difficult it seems, or how intense the situation…always remind yourself …

It's Just Retail!

Thank You and Best Wishes!

About The Author

Roger L. Tyler

Capitalizing on his (25+) years of thorough and practical business knowledge gained while working in lockstep with the decision makers and enablers within merchandising, planning, allocation, store operations, finance, distribution and information technology; **Roger Tyler** began his own consulting company in October of 2009 and began writing this book towards the later part of 2010 simultaneously. Working with a multitude of retailers, financial investment firms and manufacturers, he is able to view things from many different perspectives and resolve the most challenging of issues with the most practical, efficient and cost effective resolutions.

He credits his diversified, goal oriented business intellect and personal relationship skills to his experiences and exposure with multi-dimensional retailers operating unique business models. Roger recognized early in his evolving career that in order to become a great leader, he would first need to acquire relevant best practice principles using cutting edge technology and effectively train a diversified group of associates. Collaborative partnerships became the foundation to ensuring all business units were in tune with the objectives of the corporation. He has developed a highly effective timeline communication process to ensure the integrity and efficiencies of all interactive project teams within the merchandise area.

He is renowned for his effective uses of an empowering, participatory management style that breeds accountability, teamwork, and continuous improvement. He has garnished increased executive retail responsibility and governorship with a common objective; *"share the knowledge, reap the rewards"*. He is known for wearing multiple hats to get the job done, while retaining respect and admiration of the team for his visionary approach.

He possesses hands-on, *roll up your sleeves* experience as an architect, engineer and coach to resolving complex business issues. Manages the process of merchandise planning from end to end which encompasses the **right** forecast used to place the merchandise order, the **right** store demographic profile to quantify the order, the **right** transportation method to and from the distribution center, to the **right** time to liquidate and freshen the assortment. He couples that with thorough visionary knowledge in areas of merchandise planning, allocation, replenishment, financials, transportation and logistics.

About The Author

His channel exposure includes brick & mortar, catalog, mail order, Internet, wholesale and international within the Department, Mass, Specialty, Dollar, and Clothing retailers. He has held various decision-making leadership positions with retail bellwethers like Macy's, S&K Fashion Menswear, Family Dollar, Kmart, The Bombay Company and Fred's Inc. while cultivating his business acumen and sense of partnership early in his career with Pic N' Pay Shoes and The Federal Reserve Bank.

Contacts:
www.Linkedin.com/in/rogertyler

@Rtylers - Twitter

www.facebook.com/roger.tyler1

-Make It Happen-

INDEX

INDEX

...and then comes tomorrow...

www.ingramcontent.com/pod-product-compliance
Lightning Source LLC
Chambersburg PA
CBHW060007210326
41520CB00009B/844